KT-134-909

101 COOL MAGIC TRICKS

with Glen Singleton

HB
HINKLER
BOOKS

Cover Design: Hinkler Books Studio
Cover Illustration & Illustrations: Glen Singleton

101 Cool Magic Tricks
Published in 2004 by Hinkler Books Pty Ltd
17–23 Redwood Drive
Dingley VIC 3172 Australia
www.hinklerbooks.com

© Hinkler Books Pty Ltd 2004

10

10 09 08 07

All rights reserved. No part of this publication may be reproduced, stored in a retrieval system,
or transmitted in any way or by any means, electronic, mechanical, photocopying, recording
or more otherwise, without the prior written permission of Hinkler Books Pty Ltd.

This publication is an activity book designed to entertain children. Some activities will require
the use of materials/tools that could cause injury. Some activities will require actions that could
cause injury. The Publisher, the Editor, or their respective employees or agents shall not accept
responsibility for injury or damage occasioned to any person as a result from participation
(voluntary or involuntary) in any activity in this book, whether or not such injury, loss or
damage is in any way due to any negligent act or omission, breach of duty or default on the
part of the Publisher, the Editor, or their respective employees or agents.

ISBN: 1 7412 1742 3
Printed and bound in China

Contents

Introduction

So, you'd like to do magic tricks? Why?

If your answer is you'd like to perform in front of audiences at home or school, or even at community festivals and fetes, read on, and we'll give you some great tips to create a captivating magic show.

If you just like the idea of learning some magic tricks to do in front of your family and close friends, that's fine too. Either way, this is the book for you, because there are so many tricks—101 in fact—contained in these pages, you will be able to keep everyone entertained for months!

Magic features in the myths and legends of cultures throughout the world. You may have heard of Merlin the Magician who, it was said, trained King Arthur to become King of England more than 1,500 years ago. It was only Arthur who could pull the magic sword, Excalibur, from its rock prison (put there by Merlin), and so he became King.

Although most of us can't explain how a microchip powers our computer, or remember the principles of electricity once our science lesson is over, we readily accept what these and other marvels of technology can do for us. But who hasn't looked on in awe as a smiling magician makes a coin disappear, or reappear, seemingly at will? We love mysteries and that's the appeal of magic.

Therefore, the first rule a magician must learn is—never, ever tell anyone how to do a trick. It doesn't matter if the person is your best friend.

DO NOT TELL HOW A TRICK IS DONE!

Getting Started

There are a few rules to remember when performing magic tricks:

1 Never tell anyone how a trick is done. I know we've said this before, but it's the first rule. DO NOT TELL!

2 Practise each trick in your repertoire until you know it perfectly and can do it over and over without a mistake.

3 Keep your audience directly in front of you. Don't let people sit beside or behind you.

4 Don't repeat a trick in front of the same audience. It may be flattering to be asked to do so, but the members of your audience are really only trying to see how the trick's done!

5 As a general rule, don't tell your audience what you are going to do. It's better to let anticipation and suspense build as you perform your trick. You can, however, talk to your audience. This will help distract them, so they will not see what you are really doing!

6 Use expressions and gestures to enhance your act. For example, you can frown to show you are concentrating hard; or stand still without speaking to gain your audience's attention; or you might like to use sweeping arm gestures when you are calling upon your 'magical powers' or trying to distract your audience.

7 Make sure all your props are in perfect working order and look good—no scruffy wands or hats.

8 Once you have learnt a trick and can perform it, you may choose to alter it. This can be fun!

9 Practise and perfect the story or patter you tell while performing each trick—it's what makes you different from another person who performs the same trick.

10 Perform against a dark background under a good light.

Putting on a Magic Show

Begin by learning simple tricks that interest you and require only a few props. You will find these tricks are the easiest to perform. As you become more confident, you can learn longer, more difficult tricks.

Then it will be time to plan your act!

Every well-planned act has a beginning, a middle and an end. When planning your act, remember to place shorter tricks between longer ones, as this will help to hold your audience's interest. Think about how long you want your show to be. When you are starting out, a good show is often a short show! Maybe you only want your show to last 10–15 minutes—that's still a lot of talking and a lot of tricks when you are new to magic!

Preparation

Apart from the obvious—learning your tricks so you are really confident performing them—you need to have the props for every trick you will perform. It is a good idea to cover a table with a cloth and put the props on top of the cloth until they are needed. Make sure your props look good!

Plan what you are going to wear. Dressing up as a magician, even if you don't rely on your costume for props, is a way of really making you feel the part. You may need to wear something special for certain tricks, such as a jacket for the arm-stretching trick.

Also, if you have decided to weave a special story or line of patter throughout the show, practise this as much as your tricks. You need to be confident with everything!

7

Performing

When you are in front of your audience, act confident. Look excited about the magic tricks you are performing. Take your bows and enjoy the applause—that's one of the reasons you are there.

Speak as clearly as you can—if you mumble, your audience won't be able to follow what you are saying and may miss crucial pieces of information.

Always involve your audience by asking for volunteers and don't worry if something goes wrong. Either repeat it, if appropriate, or begin the next trick.

Plan your show so your best trick is performed last and you go out on a cheer!

Finally, have fun!

Now... I need a family member to happily step forward to volunteer for this next trick!

Quick Tricks and Simple Illusions

Begin your show with a couple of these quick and simple illusions. They will leave your audience wanting more!

1
CHAPTER

Trick 1
Long or short

★ **You need:** a pencil, a piece of paper, a ruler

This is an easy illusion to warm up your audience.

1 Draw two straight, parallel lines on the paper, making sure they are exactly the same length, say 5 cm (2 in.) each. Position them about 2 cm (1 in.) apart.

2 Then draw angles as in the diagrams below on the ends of each line. You know the lines are the same length, but it will be hard to convince your friends because an optical illusion makes one appear shorter than the other.

Step back my friends!
This is a Magic Rabbit...
...it could be loaded!

Did you know?
Mandrake the Magician was a popular comic strip hero of the 1940s. He would often outwit his opponents by using his magical powers.

Trick 2
Magical number nine

★ **You need: just a pair of hands—yours!**

It's a good idea to create a story or patter about the magical number nine for this one!

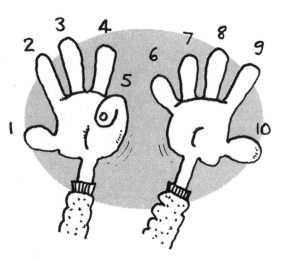

1 Did you know you can multiply by 9 easily, just using your fingers? Hold your hands up and, in your head, number your fingers from 1 to 10 starting with the little finger on your left hand.

2 Whichever number you wish to multiply by 9, bend down the finger with that number. How many fingers are left standing on either side? For example, to multiply 5 by 9, bend forward finger number 5 and count the fingers to the left and right of it. The answer is 4 on your left hand and 5 on your right hand, this is 45—correct!

3 Try it with any multiple—up to 10 of course—it works every time!

Trick 3
More nines

★ **You need:** a pencil, a piece of paper, a calculator (optional)

Keep up the illusion of nine being a magical number with this number trick.

9
18
27
36
45
54
63
72
81
+ 90
495

1 First, write down the number 9.

Then underneath, in a column, write down the multiples of 9. That is, 9 multiplied by 2, then by 3, and so on, up to 9 multiplied by 10. (You will know an easy way of doing this if you did the trick before this one!) Draw a line underneath these figures.

2 Add all the numbers together and you should get 495. Add these digits together, 4 + 9 + 5, and the answer is 18—and by adding these digits together, 1 + 8, what do you get? Yes, 9!

3 Even if you add more multiples of 9 to the column you will always end up with the same answer—9. It's a spooky number, isn't it?

Trick 4
Mind-reading

★ **You need:** a pencil, a piece of paper, a calculator (optional)

Again, this mind-reading trick uses the 'magical' number nine. Performed with the help of a friend, this trick will greatly enhance your act and impress your audience!

 Tell your friend to write down any three-digit number he likes, but the digits must decrease in value, such as 9, 7 and 2. He must not let you see what he's written.

2 Then tell your friend to write the same number backwards underneath the first—that would be 2, 7 and 9.

3 Now he must subtract this number from the first and tell you only the final digit. In our example, this is 3.

4 You will immediately be able to tell him the remaining numbers are 6 and 9, because you will subtract the 3 from the 9 to find the first digit—that will be 6. The middle digit is always 9, no matter what three-digit number your friend chose! There's that sneaky 9 again!

Trick 5

More mind-reading

★ **You need:** a pencil, a piece of paper, a calculator

Tricks that involve mind-reading and numbers are always fascinating—here's another easy and effective one to include in your show.

1 Ask a friend to write down a number. It can be any number she likes (it doesn't matter how many digits) provided the digits do not decrease in value. She is not to show you the number until the end of the trick.

15689
× 10

156890

2 Ask your friend to multiply the number she wrote down by 10. (Let's pretend your friend chose the number 15689.)

3 Ask your friend to subtract the first number from the second number.

156890
− 15689

141201

 Ask your friend to add 9 to the answer.

 Ask your friend to cross out any number she likes except for a zero. She should tell you what the remaining digits are. In our example, the second 1 is crossed out and the remaining numbers are 1, 4, 2 and 1.

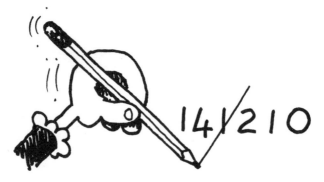

6 You add these remaining digits in your head—they come to 8—and then subtract the total from 9 to find out what number was crossed out.

7 Tell your friend the number she crossed out was 1! Mind-reading wins again!

1
CHAPTER

Trick 6

Arrows abound

★ **You need:** a pencil, a sheet of paper, a glass (straight-sided), a jug of water, a table

This magic trick is a great one to do before a small audience.

1 Fold the sheet of paper in half and draw an arrow in the middle of one side.

2 Stand the folded sheet on a table with the arrow facing the audience. Place the empty glass in front of it. Now challenge a member of the audience to turn the arrow around without touching the paper or the glass.

3 Of course, he can't do it (unless unhappily he has seen the trick done before!) but you do it by producing the jug of water (which until now has been out of sight) and filling the glass with water.

4 Hey presto! The arrow turns to face the opposite way!

Now... don't take your eyes off this cabbage for a second ... as its about to disappear!

My... what's that over there?

Did you know?
Magicians are often very theatrical performers, more so than actors! Magicians use grand gestures to distract audiences from what is really happening during a show!

Trick 7
Magic paper rings

> ★ **You need:** a paper strip about 30 cm (12 in.) by 4 cm (1.5 in.), glue, scissors

This quick little illusion will have your audience believing you can do anything!

1 Hold the paper strip and twist it once.

2 Then glue the ends together.

3 Cut around the centre of the ring carefully. What's the result? Two rings? No, it's one big ring if you've cut correctly.

4 Now to take this a little further—cut around the centre again. Do you think you'll get a really big ring this time? No! This time there are two rings!

101 COOL MAGIC TRICKS

Trick 8

Can you do it?

★ **You need:** a sheet of paper, an unopened can of food, a table

You can only show this trick once to any group as you give the game away each time.

1 Lay the sheet of paper flat on the table and put the can on top of it (right in the middle).

2 Challenge anyone in the audience to remove the paper without touching the can or allowing it to tip over. No-one will be able to do it—unless of course someone has seen the trick performed elsewhere! But you can!

3 Pick up the longer side of the paper and begin to roll it into a tube. As the paper tube reaches the can, keep rolling. Do not touch the can. The tube will move the can away from you. Keep on rolling the paper until the can has moved completely off the paper and you can wave your rolled tube in a salute!

Trick 9
Something goes!

★ **You need:** a coin, a blunt pencil

Tell your audience you can make a coin disappear—but it seems you need more practice!

1 Stand with your left side towards your audience if you are right-handed or your right side towards them if you are left-handed. Put the coin in the hand closest to the audience

and hold it up, explaining that it will disappear once you tap it sharply three times with your pencil.

2 Hold the end of the pencil with the fingers of your other hand and bring it up into the air until it is level with your ear.

ONE!

3 Bring the pencil down and tap the coin sharply with it while exclaiming a really loud "One."

4 Do this again—bringing the pencil up to exactly the same height and down again, tapping the coin and saying "Two."

THREE!

5 Without missing a beat, bring the pencil up one more time, this time sliding it easily and quickly behind your ear. Bring your now-empty hand down, saying "Three", and look really surprised to discover the pencil has vanished.

6 Turn away from the audience, without showing the pencil if possible, and mutter something about having to go and practise the trick more.

7 Remember—to succeed with this trick you need to keep the same 'beat' going when counting. Don't pause between any of the taps of the coin, especially not before the third tap!

Hey...I'm not a happy Pharoah...! What happened to the Vanishing Pyramid Trick and turning a camel into a palm tree?

Did you know?
The first record of performing magicians is in the Westcar Papyrus in the State Museum of Berlin, Germany. It contains documented proof that magicians performed for the Pharaohs of Ancient Egypt about 4500 years ago.

CHAPTER 1

Trick 10

The coin really disappears this time...

★ **You need:** a coin, a pencil, a table

This trick follows on beautifully from the previous one, but can be a stand-alone trick if you prefer.

1 Begin by sitting at a table with your side to the audience. If your dominant hand (that is the hand you do most things with) is your right hand, sit with your left hand towards the audience, and vice versa if you are left-handed.

2 Repeat trick 9 (but stay seated). When you count "Three", act surprised the pencil has vanished and look questioningly at the audience. At first they'll be surprised too, but then you should let them see the pencil stuck behind your ear and they'll begin laughing. You should laugh too.

THREE!

3 Reach up with your dominant hand to remove the pencil. Now here's the clever bit—while you are removing the pencil with one hand (and hopefully the whole audience is watching you do that), the hand holding the coin quickly tips it into your lap.

4 As the coin leaves your hand, close your hand into a fist (you want the audience to think you are still holding the coin).

5 Say something along the lines of: "Well I tricked you there, but now let me really make the coin disappear." Lift the pencil and tap your closed fist with it, then open your hand to show the coin has gone!

Trick 11
It's always 1089

★ **You need:** two pieces of paper, an envelope,
a pencil, a table, a calculator (optional)

With this quick trick you'll convince your audience you have
special powers!

1 Place your props on
the table and stand in
front of your audience. Talk
about the power of the mind—
about telepathy and thought-
reading. Say something like:
"There is always someone in my
audience whose mind is open
to me." Then stop and say
there is someone in the audience whose thoughts you are
picking up right now. Point to a person in the audience.

2 Pretend to be thinking
hard, and ask the
'telepathic' person to
concentrate on transmitting his
thoughts to you. Say you think a
number is coming through to you.
Quickly write down 1089 on a
piece of paper, place it in the
envelope and seal it.

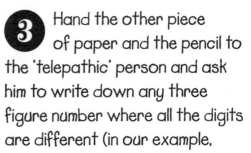

3 Hand the other piece of paper and the pencil to the 'telepathic' person and ask him to write down any three figure number where all the digits are different (in our example, we've used the number 341.) Now ask him to reverse the number and subtract the smaller from the larger one. Ask him to write down a three-digit answer even if the first digit is zero.

4 He now needs to reverse this last number and add the last two numbers together. Ask him to read his answer out loud to the rest of the audience. Now ask him to open the envelope and read the number you wrote down. Both numbers will be 1089.

5 The number is always 1089, so you only want to do this trick once in front of the same audience!

Trick 12
Pocket puzzler

★ **You need:** a deck of cards, a calculator,
a piece of paper, a pencil

Using your magical powers, you are able to name the card hidden in an assistant's pocket.

1 Ask a volunteer to come forward and write down any four-digit number on a piece of paper, without letting you see any of the numbers. The only condition is the four numbers must be different. (In our example, we'll use the number 7539.)

2 Ask him to add the four numbers together and write down the total. Now give him the calculator and ask him to subtract the total from the original number.

$$7+5+3+9=24$$

$$\begin{array}{r} 7539 \\ -24 \\ \hline 7515 \end{array}$$

3 Hand the volunteer a deck of cards and ask him to secretly remove four cards which have the same numbers as the four digits (an ace = 1 and a king = 0). Each card must be a different suit.

4 Ask your volunteer to put one card (which isn't a king) in his pocket, or out of sight, and hand you the other three cards. In our example, the volunteer puts the five of clubs in his pocket.

5 Now you must mentally add the values of the three cards. If the answer has more than one digit, add those digits until there is only one digit. (For example, 13 becomes 1 + 3 = 4).

7 + 5 + 1 = 13
1 + 3 = 4
9 - 4 = 5

6 Mentally subtract this number from 9, and the value of the card in your volunteer's pocket will appear, as if by magic! It's a five—and because you are holding cards which are hearts, spades and diamonds—the card must be the five of clubs!

7 The only exception to this clever little trick is when you mentally subtract the value of the cards from 9 and the answer is 0—the missing card isn't a king, it's a 9.

that's amazing!

Diabolically Clever Card Tricks

Many young magicians include card tricks in their magic shows. This is a good idea. Nearly every household has a deck or two of cards lying about, so no extra money needs to be spent on props, and there are many simple card tricks you can learn that look great when performed!

Trick 13
Who's lying?

★ **You need:** a deck of cards, a table

Card tricks are a magician's stock in trade. Everyone expects you to be able to flip, shuffle, twist and 'read' cards telepathically—so let's get on with it!

1 Before your audience arrives, shuffle the deck of cards—make sure you know which card is on the bottom.

2 Once your audience is seated, fan out the deck of cards on the table in front of you and ask a volunteer to choose one card. She is not to show or tell you its identity.

3 While the volunteer looks at the card, you should close the fan of cards, straighten the deck and place it on the table, face-down. Ask the volunteer to cut the deck into two equal piles.

31

4 Now ask your volunteer to put her card on the pile she cut from the top of the deck, then place the other half of the deck on top of this. This should mean the card you memorised, which was at the bottom of the pile a minute ago, is now on top of the selected card.

5 Now is the time for some good magician's patter. Explain to the audience the deck of cards is special—it can detect lies!

6 Explain to your volunteer that you are going to turn each card over and ask her if this is the card she selected. She is to say "No" every time, even when you turn over her selected card. The deck of cards will 'tell' you when she is lying. Obviously you are looking for the card you memorised—the card after it will be the selected card.

My magic pack of cards tells me you might be telling fibbies!

7 When you turn over the selected card and your volunteer says "No", yell "Liar!" loudly and watch her reaction!

Trick 14

Find the queen

★ **You need:** five playing cards (four black cards and one red queen), glue, a clothes peg

---

This trick is really an optical illusion. All your volunteer has to do is find the queen—but it's harder to do than it seems.

1 Before facing your audience you need to prepare the cards. Arrange them in an overlapping line—first, three black cards, then the red queen, then the fourth black card. Now glue them in place and leave them overnight to dry.

2 Once your audience arrives, show them the strip of cards, pointing out the red queen. Ask a volunteer to remember where it is.

3 After handing the volunteer the clothes peg, turn the cards around so the backs of the cards face the audience. Ask your volunteer to clip the clothes peg onto the queen.

4 Once he has clipped the peg onto a card, turn the strip of cards around. Your volunteer will be astonished to see his guess wasn't right because this looks so easy to do! More than likely (and you can test this yourself), the card which was pegged was the last card.

Trick 15
Balancing act

★ **You need:** one playing card, a plastic cup (not glass!)

Simple tricks are good tricks! Practise this one and you'll look like the greatest magician—and don't forget your patter. This is the story you tell while performing magic—it's exclusively yours, even if the tricks are old!

1 Hold the card with the face (that is the suit and number) towards the audience. If you are right-handed, hold it in your left hand, and if you are left-handed it should be held in your right hand. Your thumb should be on one side of the card, and the middle, ring and little fingers on the other. Your forefinger or index finger rests behind the card.

2 With your other hand, and while talking constantly to your audience about your magical powers, gently place the cup on top of the card. Place it so that three-quarters is behind the card, and move your index finger up to the bottom of the cup to hold it steady.

3 From the front it looks as though the cup is just sitting there, perfectly balanced—as indeed it is, on your finger!

Trick 16

The mysterious missing card

★ **You need:** a deck of cards (with a piece of double-sided adhesive tape on the back of the top card), a table

It doesn't matter which card your volunteer chooses from the pack—you can make it disappear immediately with this trick.

DOUBLE SIDED TAPE

 Stand facing your audience with the deck of cards in your hand. Fan out the cards between both hands, so the faces of the cards are facing your audience. (This also hides the piece of tape on the back of the top card which you've already put in place!)

2 Select one person from the audience to study the cards. Ask her to take a card from the deck.

 Once she has chosen a card, close the fan of cards and hold the deck upright, still showing the face of the cards to the audience.
If you are left-handed hold the deck in your right hand, and if you are right-handed hold the deck in your left hand.

4 While you were doing this, your volunteer should have shown everyone else the card she chose. Now you take it back with your free hand, keeping the face away from you, and place it with a flourish back on to the deck—right on top of the double-sided adhesive tape! Make sure it's squarely on top so it looks as if there is only one card there.

5 Now, place the deck face-down on the table and cut the cards. Explain to your audience that you are going to make the chosen card disappear. Say "Sim Sala Bim" or wave your hands or snap your fingers before turning over the cards and spreading them out on the table. Ask your volunteer to find the card she chose earlier. Of course, she cannot. The card has disappeared! Take a bow!

SIM SALA BIM all right! It must be some kind of trick!

6 If you prefer you can keep the cards in your hands, cut them and then count them out on to the top of the table—of course, there will be only 51 and the chosen card will have 'vanished'.

CHAPTER 2

Trick 17
The chosen card

★ **You need:** a deck of cards, a table

This trick requires some preparation, but when it's done properly, it's a real winner!

1 Separate the cards by color. Make a pile of red cards and a pile of black cards. Put one pile on top of the other, so you now have a deck of cards separated into two colored halves. Now it's time to bring on the audience!

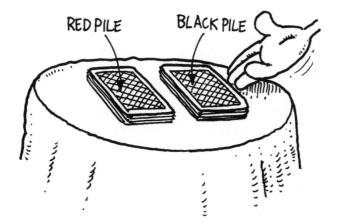

RED PILE   BLACK PILE

2 Pick up the cards and hold the deck face-down in your left palm if you are right-handed and in your right palm if you are left-handed. With your other hand, begin to flick the cards with your thumb at the end nearest you. This way, you are the only one who can see the faces of the cards. Flick upwards from the bottom of the deck. You don't

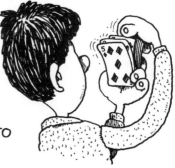

have to actually see the numbers and suits, you want to see when the colors change. While you are doing this, explain to the audience that you are going to cut the deck into two equal piles.

 Once the color changes, you stop and cut the deck. Only you know that you have cut the deck into two equal piles of different colored cards—your audience thinks you have just cut the cards into two roughly equal piles, especially when you say: "I think the piles look the same."

 Ask for a volunteer.

5 Take one pile and spread the cards face-down in your hands and ask the volunteer to take a card and remember it. He can even show it to the rest of the audience if he wants to.

6 While he is doing that, put down those cards and pick up the other pile. Spread this one out in the same way and tell the volunteer to place the selected card into this half of the deck.

7 Put the cards together again to make one deck and ask the volunteer if he would like to cut the deck. He can do this as many times as he likes. (Because your volunteer placed a card of one color into the half of the deck of a different color, it doesn't matter how many times the cards are cut. When you begin to look through the cards, you will see clusters of the same colored cards together. When you see one card of the other color in amongst these clusters, you will know this is the chosen card.)

8 However, do not let your volunteer shuffle the cards— if he does then you will not be able to find the chosen card! Also, it is possible that the chosen card will end up on the top or the bottom of the pack. If you cannot see a single card of a different color in a cluster in the deck, then check the top or bottom card. If you find a card of a different color, it is the chosen card.

Trick 18
Keep trying!

★ **You need:** a deck of cards, a table

This is one trick which relies on good patter. You need to keep your audience interested and intrigued even though you seem to be having trouble making the trick work. It also relies on good mathematics skills! Read on...

 To begin, deal three columns of seven cards. Deal them out on to the table from left to right (this is important!) and face-up. Make sure you can see the number and suit of each card. Put the rest of the cards to one side—you won't need them for this trick.

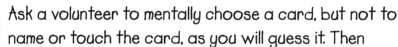

2 Ask a volunteer to mentally choose a card, but not to name or touch the card, as you will guess it. Then pretend to study the cards, as though trying to magically sense which one has been selected.

3 Tell your volunteer you seem to be having trouble magically sensing the card. Ask her to tell you which column it is in.

 When she tells you which column, pick up each of the three columns.

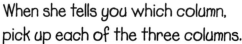

You must pick the columns up so that the column with the selected card is stacked on top of the first column, but under the third column (i.e. it's in the middle).

STEP A.

STEP B.

5 Deal the three columns again, exactly as before. Frown and pretend to be searching for the right card. You still can't find it!

6 Ask your volunteer again which column the card is in, then repeat step 4.

7 Deal the columns again. Repeat step 4.

8 By now you should be acting as though you are very annoyed! So say to your audience you will try it one last time.

9 Begin dealing the cards as before—but this time, as you are dealing, silently count to yourself until you reach the number 11. Then stop suddenly, smile with relief, and hold up the card, announcing that "This" is the selected card!

1, 2, 3, 4, 5, 6, 7, 8, 9, 10, ... 11

10 This trick depends on mathematics, so you need to follow the directions exactly. It will work every time, but it's a good idea to try it on your own to test it out!

Trick 19
The talking cards

★ **You need:** a deck of cards with no jokers, a table

You can find any card in a deck by listening to your 'talking' cards...

1 Explain to your audience that you have special powers which enable you to hear 'talking' cards—even though they won't be able to hear anything!

2 Ask a volunteer to deal out the cards face-up on the table. He must deal them out in a single row until you say "Stop." You should mentally count the number of cards being dealt, taking note of the seventh card. When your volunteer reaches 26, tell him to stop and say something like: "That should be enough cards to choose from."

3 Now tell the audience you'll select a card at random from those on the table—pretend to consider the cards, then point to the seventh card. Ask your volunteer to tell the audience the name of the selected card. Explain to your audience that you will be able to find the selected card again with the help of your 'talking' cards.

4 Pick up the cards, ensuring the seventh card stays in the seventh position. Put the cards face-down on the table in a pile and put the rest of the deck on top.

5 Slowly deal out the cards, so that they lie face-up in a column. Tell the audience the cards are 'talking' to you. Note the number of the first card. Continue to deal and silently count from that number until you reach 10. For example, if the first card is a 4, the next card becomes 5, then 6, 7, 8, 9 and 10—no matter what the numbers on the cards actually are.

6 Once you reach number 10, start another column—all the while pretending the cards are 'talking' to you. If the first card you turn over in a column is a 10 or a face-card, such as a king or queen, it counts as 10 and so you must begin the next column. Aces count as 1.

7 Make three columns and then stop. Stare at the cards and while the audience thinks you are 'listening' to the cards, you should be adding up the first cards on the table from each column, perhaps a 10, 3 and 2, which would make 15.

This number is the key to finding the selected card!

8 Now tell the audience the cards have told you the location of the selected card. Tell the volunteer to deal off the same number of cards as your total—in our example, that is 15. The fifteenth card will be your selected card! The volunteer and audience will be amazed!

9 Try this trick a few times on your own or for your parents and see how easy it is!

Trick 20
Choices

★ **You need:** a deck of cards, a table

In this trick, you ask a volunteer to deal you a card seemingly at random—but, in fact, you already know the card's identity!

 Before your show, memorise the tenth card from the top of a deck of cards.

 Begin the trick by giving a volunteer the pack of cards. Ask her to think of a number between 10 and 20, then ask her to deal that number of cards face-down into a pile on the table. The rest of the deck can be put aside.

3 Now your volunteer needs to add together the two digits that make up the number she selected. If she selected the number 14, for example, she would add 1 and 4 to get 5. She then deals that number of cards, 5, from the pile and looks at the fifth card without telling anyone what it is. This card will be the card you memorised before the trick— the original tenth card.

4 Pretend to read the volunteer's mind—perhaps you'd like to heighten the drama by drawing the card on a piece of paper, or you could ask the volunteer to return the card to the deck and shuffle the cards. She hands the deck to you and you 'select' the card by 'reading her fingerprints'!

5 However you do it, you'll be right every time!

Trick 21
ESP card

★ **You need:** a deck of cards, an envelope, a card from another deck of cards

In this trick, you hold a sealed envelope up before your audience and tell them there is a card inside. You then select a card–seemingly at random–and it matches the card inside the sealed envelope!

 Before your audience arrives, find the card (we'll call it card 1) in the full deck which matches the single card (card 2) you have taken from another deck. Place card 1 tenth from the top in the deck.

 Seal card 2 in the envelope.

3 Introduce this trick by telling your audience there is a card in the sealed envelope. Ask a volunteer to hold the sealed envelope.

4 Hand the full deck to another volunteer and ask him to select a card as in trick 20. The final card dealt will be card 1 which, of course, matches the card in the envelope.

 Ask the first volunteer to open the envelope and everyone will be sure you have special powers.

Trick 22
Topsy turvy

★ **You need:** a deck of cards, a table, a wand (optional)

Make a magician out of a volunteer with this trick. Your volunteer will pick a card, place it back in the deck, wave a magic wand—and hey presto!—the card will have magically turned over in the deck!

1 Before the audience arrives, turn over the bottom card in the deck so the deck looks the same from both ends.

2 From your audience, select a volunteer, then spread the cards out face-down on the table—taking care not to show the reversed card on the bottom of the pack. Ask your volunteer to select a card and show it to the audience, but not to you.

3 As the volunteer is showing the card to the audience, you should close the deck in the palm of one hand and secretly turn it over so that the reversed bottom card is now on top of the deck. You need to practise this movement to make it so smooth that no-one will notice you doing it.

4 Ask your volunteer to place the card face-down anywhere she likes in the deck that you are still holding. What she's done of course is place the selected card backwards in the deck of cards.

Now...say... SIM SALA BIM and let's hope it doesn't turn into a toad!

5 Now tell the volunteer she is going to perform the magic trick with the help of your magic wand (if you have one) or by speaking some magic words that you will tell her. Turn over the hand holding the deck, so it is now palm down, and put the deck of cards flat on the table. Now the deck is right-side up again with the reversed card on the bottom of the pack. The selected card is also reversed.

6 Once your volunteer has woven her magic spell over the cards, you can pick up the deck and spread the cards in a fan on the table or move them from hand to hand until you come to the selected card, which of course will be reversed face-up within the deck. Show the audience the card. Congratulate your new assistant and take the applause with her!

ONE DAY...MAGICIANS WILL PULL RABBITS OUT OF HATS AND GET PAYED FOR IT!

Did you know?

In England, in the early 1700s, magic was considered respectable entertainment. Magicians performed in private homes, at booths at village fairs and in theatres.

Trick 23
Create an image

★ **You need:** a deck of cards in its box,
a small mirror, glue, a table

This trick relies on a good set-up!

1 Before your audience arrives, glue a small make-up mirror on to the back of the box of cards. This may need to dry overnight. Keep the deck of cards in the box, with the flap closed.

2 To begin your performance, hold the box of cards in one hand with the mirror facing towards you. Remove the deck of cards with the other hand and spread the cards on the table face-down. Keep hold of the box.

3 Ask someone in the audience to choose a card, look at it, memorise it and then hand it to you. The card face must be turned away from you. (You are still holding the box and may need to make some mention of this in the patter you devise for the trick.)

4 Take the card, making sure the face is still turned towards the audience and your volunteer, and say something like: "I need the help of the magic box to sense the suit and number of the card." Then move the card behind the box so it is possible for you to glimpse the card in the mirror.

5 Keep the patter going by asking your volunteer to concentrate on the card he chose and to send a mental image of it to you. Place the box on the table (once you know what the card is!), ensuring the mirror can't be seen, and put the card on top of the box so it will release its magic powers. Then proudly tell the audience what card the volunteer chose!

6 Don't do this trick more than once before the same audience as it is too easy for someone to ask why you are holding on to the box. Someone may even see the mirror!

Trick 24

Arise card

★ **You need:** a deck of cards

Make any card you name rise out of the deck.

1 Ask a volunteer to shuffle the deck of cards.

2 When the deck is handed back to you, straighten it, taking note of which card is face-down on top. Perhaps it is the ten of diamonds.

3 Hold the deck vertically in one hand (left if you are right-handed and right if you are left-handed), so the cards are facing the audience.

PUSH ON AND UPWARDS WITH THIS FINGER

4 Place your other hand behind the deck and rest the forefinger or index finger on top of the deck. Now extend your little finger (or ring finger if it is easier) until it touches the back of the top card (the ten of diamonds).

5 Now all you need to do is name the card and ask it to rise for you! "Ten of diamonds...arise now from your slumber!" While you are saying this, push upwards on the top card with your little or ring finger, do it slowly, making sure your forefinger or index finger is rising as you speak. From where the audience is sitting it will look as if your forefinger or index finger is encouraging the rising card to rise, and it will also look as if the card is coming from the middle of the deck. Easy but effective!

Trick 25
Do drop in

★ **You need:** a deck of cards, a hat

This is another simple trick that is easy to set up and perform—it's a good one to do at the beginning of a magic show.

1 Ask for a volunteer to act as your assistant. Give your new assistant half the deck of cards.

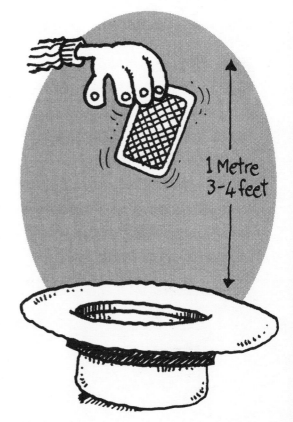

1 Metre 3-4 feet

2 Place the hat upside down on the floor in front of you. Take a card and hold it a little over 1 metre (3-4 feet) above the centre of the hat and tell your audience you bet you can get more cards into the hat than your assistant can.

3 Take a card and hold it by one end. You are just demonstrating how to drop the cards into the hat—if you actually let yours go, it probably won't go in the hat and everyone will laugh! That's OK, in fact, that's really good!

4 Now get your assistant to drop her cards into the hat one at a time. The majority of the cards will miss the hat and fall onto the floor. When your assistant has no more cards left, count the cards which have made it into the hat. Pick up the cards which didn't get into the hat and make a big noise about how poorly your assistant did!

5 Now you get to show off—and win the bet! Hold your cards flat between your fingers and thumb facing the floor. As you drop each card, the cards will fall straight down (not float and spin as before). If you are standing directly over the hat, aim for nine out of ten cards going in the hat!

CHAPTER 2

Trick 26

As many as you

★ **You need:** a deck of cards, a table, good mathematics skills!

At first, this trick may seem hard to understand. It's best to practise the trick while reading the instructions.

 1 Place the cards on the table and ask a volunteer to remove a small bunch of them. Watch and try to estimate how many cards he takes.

 2 You now take a bunch of cards yourself. Make sure it's more than your volunteer took.

3 Ask your volunteer to count his cards while you turn your back. He must count silently. While your back is turned you also count your cards silently and accurately.

4 Perhaps you have 16 cards. Now you need to use your mathematics skills. Subtract any number from 1 to 5 from your total, say you subtract 4, your new total is 12.

5 What you now say to your volunteer is: "I bet I have as many cards as you, plus 4 extra (the number between 1 and 5 you chose), and enough left over to make yours equal 12 (your new total)."

6 The volunteer tells you how many cards he has and you deal from your pile this exact number. So if your volunteer has 10 cards, you deal out 10 cards. You now say: "That's the number of cards you had." Deal 4 more cards, counting out loud, and say "That's the four extra", and finally deal out what's left in your hand. In our example, it should be 2 cards. These 2 cards plus the number of cards your volunteer had in the beginning add up to 12.

7 It sounds complicated, but the more you practise the trick on your own, the easier it will become and you'll find it works every time!

Trick 27
What's gone?

★ **You need:** a deck of cards, a table, a chair

You'll need to concentrate while performing this trick, but do it well, and you'll earn yourself a reputation as a good magician.

1 Hand one person in the audience nine cards in any suit–ace through to the number nine.

2 Ask your new assistant to shuffle the cards. While they are shuffling, you should take a seat with your back to the table.

3 Tell your assistant to deal the cards into three rows with three cards in each.

4 Now ask your assistant to remove one card, show it to the audience, then put the card in her pocket.

5 The assistant (who is really doing all the work!) now adds up the cards in the columns, ignoring the space where the removed card once was.

6 Your assistant now has to add up the digits in the answer, in our example, that would be 1 + 0 + 1 + 5 + 1 + 3 = 11. Your assistant tells you the total, which in this case is 11. Without pausing, or turning around to look at the cards or the audience, you press your fingers to your head and say: "You removed the 7."

7 You have deduced this answer on a simple mathematical basis. You always take the number given to you away from the number nine, or a multiple of nine. However, we know that 11 cannot be taken away from 9, so for any number greater than 8 you subtract it from 18. Therefore, 18 - 11 = 7—hey presto! You're right! (Should the number be greater than or equal to 18, simply subtract it from 27).

Trick 28
Card telepathy

★ **You need:** a deck of cards

If you practise and perfect this illusion, it looks really impressive, but you do need to be able to memorise a couple of cards at a time. This is a great trick to begin a show...it makes you look so good!

1 First ask a person from your audience to shuffle the deck and then hand them back to you. Explain to your audience that you will use telepathy to 'read' the card that is at the front (or top) of the pack facing them.

2 Now for the secret to your success. There are two things you do—first, you put the pack behind your back and, making sure the audience doesn't see you, you take the top card and move it to the back of the pack, so that it faces you. This will be the first card you 'guess'.

3 The next thing you do is have a 'dummy' run, by saying to everyone: "Now this is what we're going to do!" Hold the pack of cards up and explain in more detail, but don't guess the card this time. Instead you memorise the card facing you.

4 Now, begin. Put the pack behind your back and move the card you memorised to the front of the pack. Hold the pack up before your audience and correctly name the card facing them. Each time you hold the pack up to the audience, facing you is the next card you will show them and the next card you will 'guess' correctly. You must memorise it!

5 For this trick to work well, you need to play the audience along and not guess the card immediately. Pretend to be reading their minds as they concentrate on the card they can see. Say things like: "I feel it's a card with red vibrations" (or black, as the case may be); or, "It's one of the lower numbered cards in hearts" (or clubs, as the case as may be). Press the fingers of your free hand to your forehead while 'thinking'.

All these vibrations... reading minds... and deep concentration is giving me a headache!

This is the last card!

6 Around three or four cards into the trick say: "This will be the last card, because concentrating this hard always gives me a headache."

Trick 29

It's time

> ★ **You need:** a deck of cards, a watch

When you begin this trick, you might like to make references to Alice in Wonderland and the White Rabbit, who was always looking at his watch and saying, "I'm late, I'm late, for a very important date." You will use your watch in this trick.

1 Ask four volunteers to choose a card each.

2 The volunteers must then decide among themselves which of the four cards they prefer. While they discuss this, you should divide the rest of the cards into two equal piles.

3 Ask the volunteers to hand you the four cards. Do not look at the cards. Ask the volunteers which pile they want their chosen card to be placed upon. Then ask which pile they want the other three cards to be placed upon (for the trick to work, the three cards should not be in the same pile as the single card).

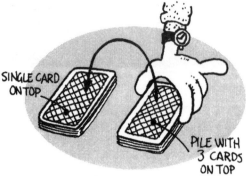

SINGLE CARD ON TOP

PILE WITH 3 CARDS ON TOP

4 Once this is done you pick up the pile with the three cards on top and place it on top of the other pile, so the single chosen card is now in the middle of the pack.

5 The reference to the time is brought in now, because you look at your watch and tell everyone it's 17 minutes past 11, for example. Ask a volunteer to add these numbers together—to get a total of 28—then deal out the cards to magically reveal the chosen card is in fact the 28th down in the pack!

Oh my.... Will you just look at the time...! 17 minutes past 11! 17 + 11 = 28 Bet your card is 28th down in the pack.

6 Of course you can only use this trick when the time will add up to 28—at 12:16, 13:15, 1:27, 14:14, 2:26, 15:13, 3:25, for example—you get the idea!

2 CHAPTER

Trick 30
Cards that spell

★ **You need:** a deck of cards, a table

Prove to your audience that cards can spell their own number! Simple, but very effective, this trick relies on the magician remembering the correct sequence when picking up the scattered cards.

1 You'll need to create some patter explaining that you've discovered cards can actually spell and you think spades (or whatever suit you choose) is the cleverest suit.

2 Once you've selected your suit take all 13 cards from the suit out of the pack. While doing this, place the 13 cards face-up on a table in a random, scattered way. If they are scattered fairly widely across the table it will seem less likely you are actually going to pick them up in a particular order. Put the rest of the pack aside.

3 Now pick the spade cards up in the following order: queen, 4, ace, 8, king, 2, 7, 5, 10, jack, 3, 6, 9. (Make sure the queen is at the top of the pack when it is face-down, and the 9 is on the bottom.)

4 Now all you have to do is have fun and remember how to spell!

5 Begin by spelling out A-C-E. When you say 'A', put the first card at the bottom of the pile, when you say 'C', put the second card at the bottom of the pile. When you say 'E', reveal the third card to be, in fact, the ace. This card is put to one side.

6 Next spell out T-W-O in the same way. Again when you get to the third card you will turn up the 2. Put it to the side on top of the ace.

7 Continue in this way spelling out T-H-R-E-E, F-O-U-R, F-I-V-E etc. until the final card left is the king.

2 CHAPTER

Trick 31

Find that card

★ **You need:** a sharp pencil, a pack of cards

In this trick you ask a volunteer to choose a card from the pack. After the volunteer has returned the card to the pack, you are able to 'magically' locate it. This is a quick and effective trick that can be placed between two longer tricks to mix up the pace.

 The secret to this trick is that you carefully run a pencil line down one side of the whole pack of cards before the performance. This line needs to be dark enough for you to see and light enough so no-one in the audience sees it!

PENCIL LINE

 Fan the pack of cards out, face-down, toward a member of the audience and ask him to select any card.

3 When the card has been selected, ask your volunteer to show it to the audience. This is your opportunity to secretly turn the whole pack around.

4 Because the pack has now been reversed, the chosen card will be the only one showing a pencil mark against the plain white of one side of the pack. With your eagle eyes and your clever patter, it is an easy thing for you to break the pack at the selected card, remove it with a flourish and show it to the audience, then wait for the applause!

The only card with a line on the other side.

Trick 32

Always red

> ★ two decks of cards with different colored designs on the back (one design should be red), a piece of paper, a pen or pencil, a table

As a magician it's great to involve your audience. In this trick you write a prediction on a piece of paper and give it to an audience member. The prediction states: "You will pick the only red card out of the six cards." And that's what happens!

1 You really only need to pick out two specific cards for this trick. One has to be the six of either hearts or diamonds and the other is the ace of either spades or clubs. The ace is taken from the deck with the red design on the back and the other five cards are from the other deck.

2 Apart from these two specified cards, the other four cards can be either clubs or spades and any value from seven up.

3 Before your audience arrives, arrange the six chosen cards in the following order at the top of the pack: other, ace, six, other, other, other.

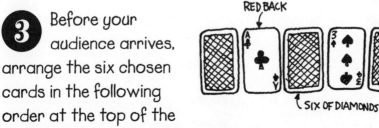
RED BACK

SIX OF DIAMONDS

4 Once the audience arrives, write your prediction down in front of them and show them. Ask for a volunteer, and as she stands with you at the table, begin by dealing out the top six cards—face-down, face-up, face-down, face-up, face-down and face-up.

5 Now the volunteer gives you a number between one and six—let's say she chooses four. Remember you've predicted she will always choose a red card, so count from right to left and you get to turn over the six of hearts or diamonds.

6 If the volunteer chooses one, you pick up the ace and show the red-backed design. If they choose two, count from left to right and show the ace again. For three, count from left to right to get to the six of hearts or diamonds. For five, count from right to left to get to the ace and for six pick up the six of diamonds or hearts straight away.

7 Don't do this trick again in the same show—it becomes too obvious you knew what cards were there first!

101 COOL MAGIC TRICKS

CHAPTER 2

Trick 33

Your card is

★ **You need:** a deck of cards

Another simple but effective trick to show you are a master
or mistress of the cards! Yet again, you will find the
'selected' card hidden in the pack, remember to deal the
cards the same way every time.

1 Deal out three piles with seven cards in each pile,
laying them out one, one, one, and two, two, two,
rather than dealing one pile at a time. Put the remainder of
the deck to one side—it won't be needed.

2 Ask an audience member to pick a card from any pile
and to remember it, but not tell anyone what it is. He
should then put the card back in the same pile.

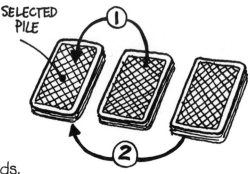
SELECTED PILE

3 You now gather up the three piles of cards, making sure the pile with the selected card is between the other two piles, then deal them out again, into three groups of seven cards.

4 Ask your volunteer to inspect each pile of cards and tell you which pile the selected card is now in.

5 Again gather all the piles of cards, keeping the selected card's pile in the middle of the other two piles, and deal them out into three groups of seven.

6 The volunteer again finds his selected card and indicates to you which pile it is now in. You gather the piles up, again keeping the selected card's pile in the middle of the other two.

Yes... don't worry... I even amaze myself!

7 Spell out Y-O-U-R-C-A-R-D-I-S by removing a card for each letter and the next card will be the selected card!

101 COOL MAGIC TRICKS

Trick 34
How odd

★ **You need:** a deck of cards, a table

This is a great trick to perform in front of young children. Many older children and adults will realise you make sure you pick up an odd number of cards—but younger children probably won't—and the trick works every time!

1 Spread the whole deck of cards out on a table and ask a member of the audience to come forward and select as many cards as she wants to, without actually looking at what she is doing. Once she's satisfied with her pile of cards, send her to one side of the stage area to count them.

2 While she is busy counting her cards, you also pick up a bunch of cards as casually as you can, but the secret is that you always pick up an odd number of cards.

3 Now tell your volunteer that whatever the number of cards she has—and you don't want to know the number—if she has an even number the cards you have picked up will make them odd, and if she has an odd number the cards you have picked up will make them even.

4 She now counts out the cards she has on to the table. You then pass over your cards and ask her to count all the cards. The new total will of course be as you predicted.

5 There are two things to remember with this little trick. You need to practise casually scooping up an odd number of cards at will—ease with this will make the trick run even better. And you don't make fun of anyone because it's so easy—especially your volunteer!

2
CHAPTER

Trick 35
Unfair deal

★ **You need:** a deck of cards, a table

Even though the cards for this trick are dealt out and regathered while you—the magician—are not looking, you can still pick which card was selected. That's magic!

1 Before the performance, put all the 4s at the top of the pack and all the 9s at the bottom of the pack. Practise shuffling so these eight cards stay right where they are.

All the 4's

All the 9's

2 Fan the cards face-down and ask a member of the audience to select one card from the pack. While your volunteer is showing the card to the rest of the audience, but not letting you know which card it is, you scoop up the remaining cards and deal them into four equal piles (one pile will have one card less than the others).

3 Now turn your back on the cards and the table and ask your volunteer to place his chosen card on one of the piles. He then puts each of the four piles of cards on top of each other in any order he likes and hands the whole deck back to you.

4 You begin to fan out the whole deck and immediately pull the selected card from the fanned cards. How did you do it? Well the secret is that once the cards are dealt into four piles, there will be a 4 on top of each pile and a 9 on the bottom of each. When you fan out the cards, the selected card will be the card which is in between a 4 and a 9.

5 You don't have to use 4s and 9s, you can use any numbers you want, but stay clear of the face-cards. When several face-cards lie next to each other, it is easier to see the trick.

Trick 36
Sticky hands

★ **You need:** a deck of cards, a ring, a toothpick, a table

This is another easy trick for young (and old!) magicians. It's easy to learn, easy to perform and easy to make look good!

1 To get ready for this trick, put on the ring. Now turn your palm so it's facing up. Slide the toothpick into the ring.

2 Place your hand carefully down on the table, making sure the audience doesn't see the

toothpick. Your patter needs to include telling the audience you are about to magically lift several playing cards with just the palm of your hand. You won't be holding on to them, they will just magically rise as you lift your hand.

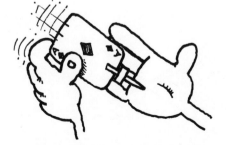

3 Take a card with your other hand and slide it under the hand on the table, making sure one end of the card slides under the toothpick.

75

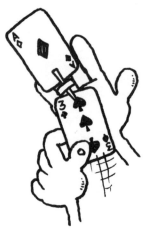

4 Pick up another card and slide it under your hand from the other direction, this time you want it between your hand and the other end of the toothpick.

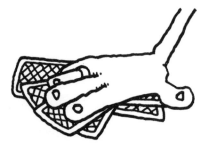

5 Try putting another four cards under your hand now, they will be held in place by the original two cards.

6 Say your favourite magic phrase—such as "Abracadabra" or "Sim Sala Bim", and slowly lift your hand with the cards horizontally above the table. The cards will stay with your hand—it's magic!

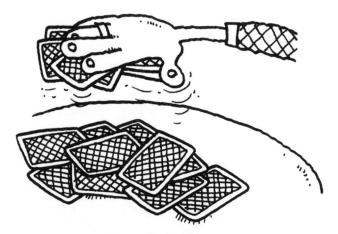

Trick 37

Gone! Into thin air

★ **You need:** a deck of cards, a handkerchief with a hem, a toothpick, scissors, a table

So you've dazzled the audience by finding the cards they've picked, but how about making cards disappear? That would be fun...

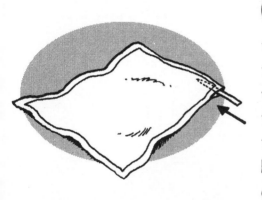

1 A little bit of preparation for this trick is necessary. Make sure the toothpick is a long as the width of a playing card—if it's too long, trim it. Now poke this toothpick into the hem of the handkerchief. You're ready for an audience!

2 Begin with a flourish by spreading the deck of cards on your table. Wave the handkerchief about and tell your audience you'll pick a card from the deck and make it vanish into thin air.

3 Lay the handkerchief over the cards so the edge with the toothpick is folded under the handkerchief.

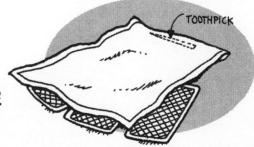

TOOTHPICK

4 Pick up the edge of the handkerchief which contains the toothpick by holding the toothpick between your thumb and index finger—it looks as if you are holding a card, right?

5 Say your favourite magic words, including something about making the card disappear. Throw the handkerchief into the air—the card appears to have vanished!

TRUE MAGIC! Look at that! NO CARD!

Cunning Coin Conundrums

Coins are easy to find around the home, so they are perfect for the budding magician to use in tricks. Of course, there are trick coins—double-headed and speciality—available at magic shops, but for most of the following tricks any coin will do!

3
CHAPTER

Trick 38

Sleight of hand

★ **You need:** one coin

All magicians learn sleight of hand. Learn this trick well and you can perform it at any time in any place—a show, a party or even a restaurant!

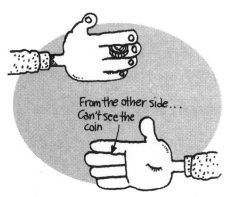

From the other side...
Can't see the coin

1 Begin by placing the coin firmly between the index and middle fingers of one hand. The coin should be hidden, so that when *you* present your open hand (palm out) to the audience they can't see a thing.

2 Now we come to the part that *you* need to practise and practise. To produce the coin you turn your fingers in towards the palm of your hand and use your thumb to bring the coin to the front.

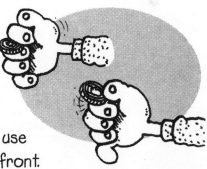

Juliet, Here art thou Romeo...

You're no Magician!!

GET OFF!

We want MAGIC!

Did you know?
By the 1800s, magic was often performed in theatres in many countries. At some venues, magicians performed regularly.

Trick 39

Spin that coin

> ★ **You need:** a coin (with a textured edge),
> two pins, a table

This is so simple, it's not really a trick. In fact, anyone can do it, but you're the one who has practised and practised to make sure it works every time!

1 Place the coin on the table and pick it up gently between the points of both pins.

2 Once you're sure it's secure, blow really gently on the coin and it will begin to spin.

3 That's all there is to it! It's a great trick to open a small magic show, you only need to keep the coin spinning for a few seconds—or longer if you like—to ensure that the audience thinks you're a great magician!

3

CHAPTER

Trick 40

Where's my coin?

★ **You need:** a ball of yarn, a special coin slide,
a coin, a glass, a table

It's time to make a coin disappear, then reappear! A bit of
preparation is needed for this trick—you need to make a
metal slide to ensure the coin reaches the inside of the ball
of yarn—otherwise no trick!

1 Before your audience arrives, wind a
fairly loose ball of yarn and prepare
the metal slide—it can be a flat piece of tin
or a small, but wide, metal ruler. Make sure the

metal slide can slide easily into the ball of yarn. You will use it
to put the coin inside the yarn. Place both props on your
table, but out of sight of your audience. The slide should be
part of the way into the ball of yarn.

2 Borrow a coin from an audience member (you
should have a coin on hand in case no-one has
one!) and hold it carefully between the tips of the
thumb and index fingers of your left hand.

3 Bring your right hand over your
left hand as if to take the coin,
but as soon as your right hand shields
the coin from the audience's sight, let the
coin drop into the palm of your left hand.

4 As the coin drops, close your right hand into a fist as if you are holding the coin and move it away to the right, making sure you follow your right hand with your eyes, so the audience will look there too. As you do this, just let your left hand fall down to your side quite normally.

5 While you are doing all this, of course you are chatting to your audience. Talk about how quickly money disappears these days—here one minute, gone the next. As you get to this part of your patter, open your right hand slowly and appear astonished that the coin has vanished.

6 At the same time, reach for the ball of yarn with your left hand and drop the coin into the slide. Push the coin into the ball of yarn, then pull the slide free. It sounds like a lot to do while you are continuing to chat to your audience about how money seems to vanish so quickly, but with lots of practice you'll be amazed at how good this part of the trick can look!

7 Now show the audience the ball of yarn, place it in the glass and unravel it gently. The coin will clink into the glass. Now, hand the coin back to the person you borrowed it from and ask if it's the same coin. Of course, it is, and everyone's impressed!

3 CHAPTER

Trick 41
The coin fold

★ **You need:** a coin, a small piece of paper

Another easy but effective trick using just one coin—
especially suitable for a small audience.

1 Place the coin in the centre of the piece of paper.

2 Fold the bottom edge of the paper up and over the coin, leaving a 6 mm (0.25 in.) gap between the two edges of the paper.

3 Fold the right edge of the paper back behind the coin.

4 Then fold the left edge of the paper back behind the coin.

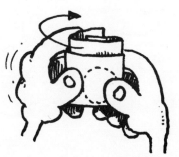

5 Make the final fold by bending the top flap of the paper back behind the coin. It seems as if the coin is completely wrapped, but in fact the top edge is still open.

6 You now turn the package around so the open edge allows the coin to slip into the palm of your hand, where it stays while you 'prove' the coin has disappeared by tearing up the paper package.

WOOPS!

Did you know?

Harry Houdini (Ehrich Weiss was his real name) is still the best known magician. He was known as an escapologist and his catchcry was No Jail Could Hold Him! He often performed outdoors too, which added to the drama. He escaped from a straightjacket while hanging by his ankles tied high above a street—he received plenty of publicity for that trick!

Trick 42

"Now you see it, now you don't!"

★ **You need:** two sheets of the same colored paper, one sheet of paper in another color, a glass, glue, scissors, a coin, a wand (optional)

Actually the saying needs to be reversed for this disappearing and reappearing coin. Read on!

1 Before the show begins, make the magic cone by rolling the single sheet of colored paper. Glue it in place and add stars and glitter to make it look magical.

2 Next, cut out a circle from one of the other colored sheets using the glass as your guide, and glue it to the rim of the glass. This will cover the coin and will not be seen as it will be resting on a sheet of the same colored paper. Put the magic cone, glass and coin on the sheet of colored paper. Now you're ready for your audience.

GLUE

PAPER

PAPER GLUED ON

3 Tell your audience the cone is endowed with magic powers and can make things disappear. You will make the coin disappear.

4 Cover the glass with the cone and place it over the coin. Tap the cone with a wand or simply wave your hands about saying magic words, such as "Abracadabra!"

5 Lift up the cone to show the glass, but no coin—it has been magically spirited away.

6 Of course the coin is really still on the table, but because the same colored paper that covers the rim of the glass is under the glass, it appears the coin has gone. Therefore it's easy for you to be a really clever magician and restore the coin to the table by reversing the process. Place the cone over the glass again, use a few simple magic words and a flourish of hands, and pick up the cone and the glass, and there it is—the coin has reappeared!

I HAVEN'T GOT TIME FOR MAGIC I'M TOO BUSY DRIVING ROUND THE UNIVERSE!

Did you know?

Popular magicians took their travelling shows around the world. Early in the twentieth century, one American magician had his Wonder Show of the Universe touring the world. He was America's top performer for 30 years.

Trick 43
Where's that coin?

★ **You need:** a handkerchief, a coin, Blu-Tack, a table

In this trick, a coin is placed in the centre of a handkerchief in full view of an audience—the magician weaves a magic spell—and it's gone!

1 Before facing your audience, stick a small piece of Blu-Tack to one corner of the handkerchief. This needs to be kept hidden from the audience at all times during the performance.

2 Spread the handkerchief out on the table, keeping hold of the corner which has the Blu-Tack. Place the coin in the centre of the handkerchief and immediately cover it with the corner with the Blu-Tack.

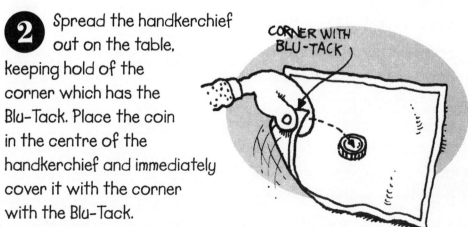

CORNER WITH BLU-TACK

3 Fold the other three corners into the centre of the handkerchief over the coin.

4 Place the fingers of both of your hands under the folded edge of the handkerchief which is nearest you. Because of this quick move the coin, stuck to the handkerchief, ends up in your hand.

5 Show both sides of the handkerchief to the audience, give it a quick shake and put it in your pocket to finish. Or pretend to blow your nose on it, or pretend to sneeze and cover your nose and mouth with it—anything for a good finale and a round of applause!

6 Perhaps you would like to make this coin reappear? It can be done, of course it can, it's magic! Or it's good planning. Simply have an identical coin hidden somewhere strange—down the top of your sock maybe, or when you remove the coin from the handkerchief keep it in your hand and then produce it from anywhere you like. Maybe from behind the ear of one of your audience members?

Great...I need a hanky to blow my nose!

Trick 44
The chemical coin

★ **You need:** one coin, a table, a chair

You'll also need some good patter and it's best to perform this intriguing trick before a small audience.

1 Your story should begin as soon as the audience arrives. Talk excitedly about what you've just read on the Internet—that chemicals in the human body can degrade the metals which make up a coin—in fact, coins can just disappear!

2 Show the coin to your audience and sit down at your table resting your chin on your right hand. Begin rubbing the coin held in your left hand against your right forearm, making sure no-one can actually see the coin as you do this.

3 While you are rubbing the coin on your arm, continue telling the fantastic story you began your show with, and now the coin should slip out of your left hand and drop on to the table. Continue with the story and make sure you are looking at your audience.

4 Pick up the dropped coin in your right hand and pretend to pass it back into your left hand, but you actually keep it in your right hand.

5 Prop up your chin again in your right hand and pretend to rub the coin on your forearm as before. This movement must be done really masterfully and you must continue on with your story while this happens.

6 Keep on rubbing for a little longer, then suddenly look a little concerned, continue to rub— maybe even a bit harder—and then slowly stop the rubbing, lifting your left hand fingers one at a time.

At the same time, you carefully drop the coin into your shirt collar, then, with a flourish, show your audience the coin has disappeared, just as you predicted!

3
CHAPTER

Trick 45
Holey napkin

★ **You need:** a coin, a cloth napkin, a black marker pen

This is a very impressive trick—easy to do and great to watch!

1 Your audience must be seated directly in front of you, as with most tricks! Ask a volunteer for a coin or hand over yours and ask the volunteer to mark it with the marker so it will be recognisable later on.

2 Hold the coin upright between the thumb and index finger of your left hand.

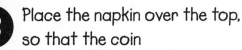

3 Place the napkin over the top, so that the coin is in the centre of the cloth.

4 Now for the tricky bit—carefully arrange a small fold of the napkin between your thumb and the coin. With your right hand, lift the front of the napkin and drape it back over the top of the napkin and over your left wrist.

COIN
FOLD

5 Make a point of showing your audience the coin is still there.

COIN

6 Continue to hold both the coin and the napkin, then flick your left wrist forward which will make both halves of the napkin fall forward.

7 Now twist the napkin so it appears the coin is wrapped securely inside. Place a little pressure on the edge of the coin and it should rise magically up through the napkin— or that is how it will appear to your audience!

3
CHAPTER

Trick 46

The coin tells

★ **You need:** four coins of different values, a table

You'll be amazed at how simple this trick is—don't forget to learn some good patter to ensure your audience is really convinced it's magic!

1 Place the four coins on the table while talking about telepathy. Ask an audience member to choose a coin while your back is turned. Tell her to hold it tightly and concentrate hard so you can pick up the vibes from her mind!

2 Concentrate silently for a few moments, pretending you are trying to pick up thought-waves, but what you're really doing is slowly counting to 30.

3 When you reach 30, say dispiritedly that you aren't receiving any thoughts from her and accuse her of not concentrating hard enough. Whatever she says, ask for the coin to be put back on the table with the others while you're still not looking, and say that you'll get the coins to tell you which one was selected.

4 Turn around and pick up each coin in turn and hold it up to your ear to 'hear' the coins 'talking' to you. What you're really doing is feeling each coin, because the one which has been held by your volunteer will be much warmer than the others.

5 So, once you find the warmest coin, show it to the audience and wait for the applause!

I HEARD THIS ONE SAY...
IT'S ME... IT'S ME!

CHAPTER 3

Trick 47
The weeping coin

★ **You need:** a coin, a small piece of wet (but
not dripping) sponge

An emotional, crying coin? Whatever next!

SPONGE

1 Before your audience arrives, wet
the piece of sponge and make sure
it fits between the coin and your thumb
without being seen by the audience. It
must hold enough water to allow you to
make the coin 'cry' tears.

2 Once the audience is there, hold up the coin between
your thumb and index finger (keeping the wet sponge
hidden with your thumb) and tell them a really good story
about how some coins are very emotional and you bet you
can get this one to cry!

3 Now squeeze the sponge
gently, while you yell at the
coin. Tears should begin to flow!

OH.../ WHAT A
SAD LITTLE COIN!
DID I MAKE YOU CRY?

4 Once the tears stop, put the
sponge and coin in your pocket.
If a member of the audience wants
to check the coin is real, just pull it
out again—minus the sponge of course.

Trick 48
Snatch!

★ **You need:** a coin

Again, a simple coin trick which makes the magician look very, very clever! The idea is to put a coin in the palm of your hand and challenge a volunteer to snatch it from you before you can close your hand. Your volunteer can't do it, but when you switch places, you get the coin on your first try.

 1 OK the audience is here. Put the coin on your palm and keep it flat.

 2 Your volunteer now tries to grab the coin before you close your hand—be as quick as you can. Your volunteer will fail every time.

 3 Now swap. Your volunteer must hold the coin in exactly the same way as you did—flat on the palm of his hand.

 4 How do you do it? OK, place your fingers and thumb together, without touching, and make sure these fingers are pointing down toward the coin.

5 Quickly move your hand down, gently striking the palm of your volunteer's hand with your fingertips. This action means the volunteer's hand will be pushed downwards a little, and the coin will jump up into your waiting fingers! Try it! It works!

Classic Conjuring

Every magician needs to spend some time
perfecting a few classic magic tricks. Don't worry
if some of the tricks seem old-fashioned or so well
known you think everyone will know how they're
done—it's what you say and how you perform them
that your friends will love. You'll probably think of
a new way to do one or more of them anyway—
that's OK—magic doesn't stay the same.

Trick 49
Long arm

★ **You need:** nothing–just your arm!

Perhaps not a classic trick, but a classic effect. People love seeing a magician do something they don't think they can do themselves...

1 You'll need to practise this trick over and over again– try doing it in front of a mirror so you can see the effect you are trying to create. You do need to wear a jacket or a coat while performing (and practising) this trick.

2 First, stand still and bend your arm so your left hand and wrist is level with your waist.

3 Now, pinch the loose skin on the back of your left hand near the knuckle of the middle finger with the other hand.

CHAPTER 4

4 Shake this skin loose a little and as you do it appears you're actually stretching your arm by tugging it out of its sleeve to an abnormal length. That's all there is to this trick, but it's so effective when done really well and with a great story, for example:

PRESS SLEEVE AGAINST YOU HERE

"The bloke you met in Longreach, Australia...boy, did he really have a long reach!"

5 Once you've pulled out the really long arm, you can tap your arm back inside the jacket sleeve as part of the story.

6 The effect is created by hugging the jacket or coat sleeve tightly to your body as you move your arm a normal length—don't let the audience see your elbow just above the hem of the sleeve or you'll give the game away!

Trick 50

Where's my thumb?

★ **You need:** just your hands

This trick takes much longer to read through, than do! But you'll need to practise for several weeks before you'll be ready to perform it. You want your audience to believe the tip of your left thumb is being magically removed—without any blood!—from your hand.

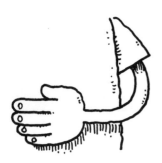

1 How do you do this? Begin by holding your left hand in front of you, at about waist height. The palm of your hand faces towards you, your fingers are flat and pointing to the right. Make sure your thumb is on the same line as your index finger.

2 Pretend to pull the top off your left thumb with your right thumb and index finger. Make a big deal of this with lots of grunts and groans and twisted facial expressions! Of course you can't do it, can you?

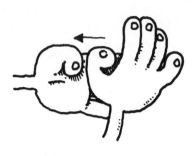

3 Well maybe you can! Try again, and this time, as you place your right index finger over the left thumb joint, bend the top of your left thumb down and put your right thumb so it looks as if it has replaced it.

4 Well, if you thought that was difficult, wait until you try this part! Tuck the other fingers of the right hand away so the audience can clearly see your right thumb tip–which of course now looks as if it is your left thumb tip! Got it? Good!

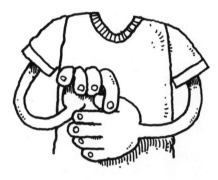

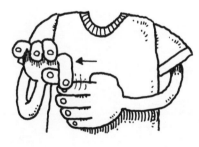

5 To complete the illusion, and with your audience going "Argh!", keep your left hand still and slowly slide the right thumb along the top of your left index finger. Then slowly slide it back to the original spot.

6 When your thumbs touch, bring back the fingers which were screening the join and show your hands with thumbs intact to your audience! Take a bow!

Trick 51
Silky hanky

★ **You need:** a small rubber band, a large patterned
silk square, a ring, a table

This is a simple trick you can do practically anywhere—
great for entertaining young children and adults alike! Show
them you can make a ring disappear!

1 Before facing your audience, slip a
rubber band over three of the fingers
on your left hand.

2 Once your audience arrives, take out
your silk hanky and wave it about using your
right hand so all eyes are on it
and not on the rubber band
over your fingers! You don't
want your audience to
notice the rubber band.

3 Spread the hanky over
your left hand with a
flourish and secretly slip your
thumb into the rubber band to
widen it a little more.

4 Ask your audience if you can borrow a ring (of course, if they haven't got one you already happen to have one on your table!).

5 Show everyone the ring and then place it on the silk hanky above the rubber band. With your free hand, rub the ring saying a magic chant. Of course what you are doing is pushing the ring through the band into a fold of silk below.

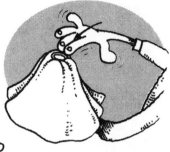

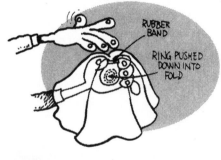

6 Slip the band off your fingers to trap the ring in a fold in the silk while making a dramatic gesture and saying more magic words.

7 Dramatically whip the hanky away with your right hand and look amazed to see that the ring has disappeared from your left hand.

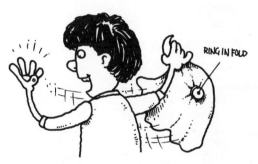

RING IN FOLD

8 Return the ring by spreading the silk over your left hand again, reach into the folds with your right hand and pull out the ring with a smile!

Trick 52

See-through hand!

★ **You need:** your hands, a coin

This trick will entertain everyone when you perform it smoothly and with lots of great acting!

1 Make a fist with your left hand and hold the coin above it in your right hand.

2 Tell your audience that you intend pushing the coin right through your hand. Begin pushing the coin down between the fingers of your left hand.

3 As it goes, it will slide out of sight behind your fingers, so you can proudly announce that it's 'gone through' your hand.

COIN PUSHED IN BETWEEN FINGERS

4 You open your fist but there is no coin, so you have to pretend you think it's stuck halfway! Ask your audience where they think it is—there will nearly always be people who think they know!

5 Try again and this time add the tricky bit. As you turn your left hand back over into a fist, your thumb nearly touches the fingers holding the coin. Just as this happens, let the coin slip down from your fingers into your left hand at the same time as you make it into a fist again.

6 Because you've practised and practised, it all goes smoothly. The audience will tell you they think the coin is still hidden by your fingers somehow. Say you'll push harder this time, and then slowly turn your fist and open it up to reveal the coin!

Trick 53

The classic scarf trick

★ **You need:** a long silky scarf, a high-necked top

Most of the classic tricks are very simple, just like this one. The real trick for a magician—young or old—is to be smooth and professional!

1 Prepare for this trick by tucking the silky scarf into the neck of your high-necked top at the front and sides only.

2 In front of your audience, hold the ends of the scarf securely and pull both ends forward on the count of three, or perhaps while chanting "Sim Sala Bim!"

3 To complete the illusion, pull the scarf forward in one quick motion so it appears to pass straight through your neck! Wait for the applause!

Did you know?

Harry Houdini died in agony after a student, who had heard he could withstand a powerful blow to the stomach, punched Houdini before he was ready. He was taken to hospital and died a few days later.

101 COOL MAGIC TRICKS

Trick 54
The magic cone

★ **You need:** a paper cone with a secret pocket, a silk hanky

It's worth finding a special cone, or making your own for this trick, as it's likely to be one of the best tricks you do. Tell your audience you will make a silk hanky disappear.

1 Unfold the cone so your audience can see it's just a cone (but we know better!) with one decorated side and one plain side.

2 Fold it back into a cone shape and push the silk hanky into the secret pocket.

3 Speak some magic words and clap your hands together, flattening the cone and the silk in the pocket!

4 Unfold the cone carefully and show that there is nothing on the front or back of it—the hanky has gone!

CHAPTER 4

Trick 55

How eggstraordinary!

★ **You need:** an egg, a pencil, a silk handkerchief, a teaspoon, an egg cup (optional)

Done well, with lots of clever chat, this trick will make your audience truly believe you can pull a handkerchief out of an egg.

1 First, prepare the egg. Make a hole in the side of an uncooked egg. Gently spoon out the contents of the egg—have scrambled eggs for tea! Wash the shell inside and let it sit and dry naturally. Remember to be careful while doing this. Once the shell has dried, carefully poke your silk hanky into the hole with a pencil.

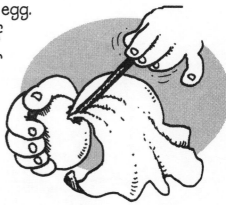

HOLE AT BACK

2 Now the clever thing is to convince your audience you have lost your hanky, but you're going to eat an egg instead. Of course they will think it's a boiled egg, so when you hold it up in the air for the audience to see, keeping the hole towards you, you could pretend it's hot.

3 Now, pop the egg back on the table and tap it gently with your spoon, then gasp and say something like: "How eggstraordinary! You'll never guess where I've found my hanky."

4 Break the egg apart excitedly and pull out the hanky, waving it in the air.

Trick 56
How many balls?

★ **You need:** three small sponge balls

To do this trick, you'll need to learn a new skill—it's called palming.

1 First, you need to learn to palm the sponge balls—at least they aren't very large! Place one ball in the palm of your hand. Bring your thumb over a little way to hold it in position, it shouldn't move, even when you hold your hand upright. Practise until you can keep the sponge ball in place when you are moving your hands around a lot. Now try to palm two balls!

2 Once you are really good at palming, you're ready to move on to the next step, which is tricking an audience.

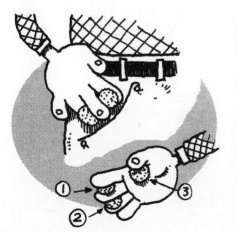

3 Have all three balls in your pocket before you begin your performance. Tell the audience you are getting two balls out of your pocket. Show the audience the two balls in your right hand.

However, you have already palmed a ball, so there are really three balls in your right hand, but the audience must see only two of them.

4 Tell the audience you are moving one ball to your left hand. While you move the ball, secretly move the third ball to your left hand too.

5 Now hold two balls up in the air, one in each hand, and ask your audience to agree that you have one ball in each hand. They of course will agree, and then you pass the ball

from your right hand to your left hand, saying as you do: "Of course, now I have two balls in my left hand, don't I?"

6 But of course you don't—there are three balls nestling in your hand.

7 Palming skills will come in very handy throughout your magic career—learn to do it well!

OF COURSE IT'S A REAL GRENADE... EVERYTHING IS REAL IN MAGIC!

Did you know?

During the Second World War, many magicians entertained the troops. Magicians travelled overseas as well as performing on home ground.

Trick 57
Together forever!

★ **You need:** a five dollar bill, two paper clips

This is another simple trick. It may take a while to perfect, but when it is performed well, it's a winner! Tell your audience you can make two paper clips link up without touching them.

1 Stand directly in front of your audience and fold the five dollar bill into a Z shape.

2 Place the paper clips on the folded bill.

3 Hold up the five dollar bill so the audience can see what it looks like and then warn the front row of the audience they may have to duck!

4 Now carefully hold the five dollar bill at each end and quickly snap it back into a straightened position. The paper clips will link themselves together and possibly fly right out into the audience!

5 Stand by for loud applause.

Trick 58
The spinning egg

★ **You need:** eleven fresh eggs,
one hard-boiled egg, a table

Whatever you do, don't drop any of the fresh eggs!

1 Prepare for the trick by hard-boiling an egg. And then, when the egg cools, place it back in the egg carton with the fresh eggs, making sure you remember its position.

2 Once you are in front of your audience, pass out the eggs to eleven volunteers in the audience, keeping the hard-boiled one for yourself.

3 Using your egg (which no-one but you knows is hard-boiled), show them how to spin an egg. Obviously you need to practise first!

4 Then invite you eleven volunteers up one by one to try to spin their eggs. No-one will be able to do this little trick because a fresh egg won't spin.

5 Actually, it's even more fun if there are two hard-boiled eggs in the carton, because then one of the volunteers really will be able to spin an egg and then you can make a really big deal out of it!

Trick 59
Cups and balls

★ **You need:** three cups, four small sponge balls, one larger sponge ball

This may be the oldest magic trick—hiding a ball under a cup! Magicians all over the world learn it to entertain and confuse their audiences.

The special cups used in this trick can be purchased wherever magic props are sold; consider buying a set of clear plastic cups to begin with, so you can see exactly where each ball is as you learn. Each cup has a rim which prevents another cup being pushed completely inside it, enabling a ball to be hidden in the space created. Also, the bottom of each cup has an indent which allows a soft sponge ball to rest without rolling off.

1 To prepare, place the large ball in your left pocket and one small ball in each of the three cups, and the fourth small ball in your left hand. The cups are then placed inside each other. They should be sitting mouth-up.

2 When you begin the performance, turn each cup over quickly, keeping the ball hidden underneath.

3 Tap or wave your hand over all the cups and then lift the right-hand one (with your right hand) showing a ball resting on the table underneath it. Transfer the cup to your left hand, so it covers the small ball hidden there.

4 Repeat with the other two cups, showing the two other balls, and sitting the cups on top of the one already in your left hand.

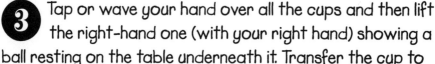

5 Now place each cup mouth-down directly behind each ball on the table. Place one first to the right and then the left, so the first cup now becomes the central cup. As you place this cup on the table, make sure the concealed ball drops into it as you turn it upside down.

6 Pick up one of the balls and place it on top of the central cup. Next place both the other cups on top and with a tap or wave of your hand, lift all three cups as one to reveal a ball on the table. To the audience it appears as though you have magically made the ball pass through the base of the cup. Wait for the applause...and then say: "But wait, there's more!"

4
CHAPTER

7 Again separate the cups and place them mouth-down on the table, this time putting the cup which contains the extra ball in the middle over the ball already on the table. Place a ball on top of this cup and repeat step 6. The difference could be that you invite an audience member to tap the cup—while your volunteer is doing this, you take the large ball from your pocket, holding it in your left hand.

8 Again lift all three cups as one and, astonishingly, all three small balls are on the table. Casually place the cups over your left hand and act as though the trick is finished by placing all three cups (and the larger ball) on the table.

9 A bit of acting here will earn you enormous applause, so hesitate as if you want to tell your audience something, but shouldn't. Then say you'll reveal a magic secret—you did use more than three balls for the trick! Pick up the cups to reveal a much larger ball—to more applause!

THANKYOU!
THANKYOU!
THANKYOU!

Masterly Mental Magic

A magician can gain much by learning a few mentally challenging tricks. They always work and they always make the magician look, well, magical!
Many are card tricks, many need a little bit of preparation, and of course they all need practice, but it's worth the trouble as they are all terrific tricks to perform.

5 CHAPTER

Trick 60
Colors in your life

★ **You need:** six index cards, a black marker pen, a table

Keeping the audience's attention on the great names of colors you have chosen will distract them from the simplicity of this trick!

1 A little preparation is necessary for this trick. Write the name of a different color on each index card, and be creative with the names of the colors because you have to have a different number of letters for each color.

LAVENDER   BLUE
RED   GREEN
YELLOW   MAGENTA

2 Perhaps you would have red (3) and blue (4), followed by green (5) and yellow (6). These are fairly straightforward colors, but how about magenta (7) and finally, lavender (8 letters).

3 Now you're ready for your audience. Place the cards randomly on a table with the names of the colors facing up and ask a volunteer to pick a color.

4 Your volunteer is not to tell anyone the name of the color, but must silently spell the name of the color, one letter at a time, as you touch each card. When your volunteer reaches the last letter of the color, he must say "Stop" and your hand will be resting on the correct card!

5 How it works? Well, for the first two letters you touch any card at all, then with the third letter you touch the three-letter color, with the fourth letter the four-letter color card and so on. You will always be on the correct card when the audience member says stop!

Trick 61
Whacky clock

★ **You need:** a photocopy of a large clock, a pencil

Find a really great clock face to
photocopy, because the more
zany it is the more it will
distract your audience from
the simple, but clever, trick you
are about to do for them.

1 Ask a volunteer to look at
the photocopied clock face
and select a number from it—silently! Ask your volunteer to
add 1 to the number she selects, so if she chooses 7, she
adds 1 to make 8, keeping this all in her head.

2 If she needs to write
down the number she
first thought of, let her do so,
but make sure you can't see it.

3 Now for the clever bit! Ask your volunteer to begin
counting silently from the number she now has (so the
next number is 9) each time you tap your pencil on the
clock's face.

4 When she gets to 20, she is to say "Stop!" Remarkably, you will be on the correct number so you circle it on the clock's face and hand it to your volunteer face-down. She is to tell the audience the number she originally selected and then turn over the page to reveal your answer. Your answer will be correct every time!

ANTI-CLOCKWISE FROM 6

5 The secret? Well, it is that you begin tapping on the clock's face at the number 6 each time you do the trick and you tap anti-clockwise on the numbers. When your volunteer says stop after reaching 20, you will always be on the correct number—it's magic!

6 If you are going to repeat this trick in front of the same audience, make sure no-one sees where you begin tapping each time.

Trick 62
Plus and minus

★ **You need:** a piece of paper, a pencil

This is an easy one if your mathematics skills are good. You can't use a calculator–it just doesn't look as impressive!

1 Ask a member of your audience to write down a five figure number on the piece of paper. The number must be made up of five different numbers–no two numbers can be the same. Your volunteer keeps this piece of paper and his workings hidden from you at all times. For example, the number might be:

2 Now ask him to reverse the number, write it underneath the first number and subtract the second from the first number.

3 You now need your volunteer to reverse this number and write it down underneath the previous number and this time add them together.

4 Once he says he has an answer, you as the magician must act up a storm, saying you can read his mind and know the number he has arrived at. It will nearly always be 109 890—occasionally it will be 99 099. If you are wrong on the first guess of 109 890, always blame bad vibes and say, "Ah, it's coming to me now—it's 99 099!"

CHAPTER 5

Trick 63

Famous names

★ **You need:** ten cards big enough to write names on but small enough to fit into the magic hat, a pencil, a piece of paper, a hat

You'll choose the correct name every time, but you can only do this trick once per audience!

1 Ask people in your audience to call out ten famous names. And as they do, write each name on a card and place it in the hat. Well, that's what your audience thinks you're doing! What you are really doing is repeatedly writing down the first name called, perhaps it was Nelson Mandela. Write that on a card, place it in the hat, and pretend to write down the next nine names called out—maybe you'll hear Madonna, Tom Cruise, Shakespeare and Kylie Minogue and others shouted out—but every time you write down Nelson Mandela and put the card in the hat!

2 Now of course it's easy. You ask someone from the audience to come up and pick a name out of the hat, read it but not tell anyone.

3 You ask your volunteer to concentrate hard on the name and *you* do the same, making sure you act as if it is very hard to do! After a few seconds of this tell the audience you now believe you can read the volunteer's mind and the answer is "Nelson Mandela."

4 Everyone will be astounded and cheer and clap wildly. On no account are you to repeat this trick with the same audience—for obvious reasons!

Trick 64
Mystery mathematics

★ **You need:** a piece of paper, a pencil

You'll always astonish your audience with your clever number skills with this trick and you only have to remember one thing.

1 Ask an audience member to call out a single digit number (that is, a number from 1 to 9). You write it on the piece of paper and show it to the audience.

2 Now you take that number, double it, add 4, then divide by 2 and finally subtract the original number. For example, if the number called out was 3; double it to get 6; add 4 and you have 10; divide by 2 and you get 5; subtract 3 and the answer is 2.

3 You need to predict the answer to astonish your audience, and you always can once you (or your audience) have chosen an adding number. That number can change each time you do this trick and the answer will always be half of that number. In the above example you added 4, so you can immediately write down the answer as 2 before you continue with the trick. It makes it even trickier if you ask an audience member to shout out an adding number—you know the answer will always be half of this number.

4 Change the adding number and have a few attempts—it's one where the audience rarely guesses how the trick works, even though it's so simple!

Trick 65
They match!

★ **You need:** two pieces of paper, two pencils

In this simple but effective trick, your volunteer is in on the secret! You tell the audience that your powers of mental concentration are so good that you will be able to write the same sentence as someone from the audience—just using the extraordinary powers of your mind!

1 Ask a volunteer from the audience to write down a sentence on one of the pieces of paper—it can be anything your volunteer likes. Your volunteer then folds the paper and hands it on to another member of the audience.

2 Put the other piece of paper in front of you and tell the audience you are going to write the same sentence. This is the time to use those acting skills as you pretend to be concentrating hard. Write down "You're right, they match!" on your piece of paper. Fold it and hand it to the same person who is holding the sentence written by the volunteer.

YOU'RE RIGHT, THEY MATCH!

Ask this person to open the volunteer's piece of paper and read the sentence out aloud.

 Now ask this person to open the paper containing the sentence you wrote and read it out aloud. The reader will laugh (of course!) and then say, "You're right, they match!" because that is what is written on the paper!

 You audience will be tremendously amazed and clap and cheer, until the reader tells them the truth!

Trick 66

Secrets? What secrets?

★ **You need:** two pieces of paper, a pen or pencil

People who use calculators to do their arithmetic may find this trick a bit hard. You need to calculate everything on paper unless you can find a calculator which has room for a ten-digit answer!

1 Begin by asking for a volunteer to help you with this trick.

2 Give him a piece of paper and a pen or pencil and tell him he is going to do some silent calculations. Then, just by looking at these calculations, you, the magician, will be able to tell the volunteer's phone number and age!

3 First of all the volunteer writes down his phone number on the paper, then multiplies it by two (see the example). Now ask him to do the following: add five to the total, then multiply it by 50, add his age, add 365 and finally subtract 615.

$$
\begin{array}{r}
92879192 \\
\times\ 2 \\
\hline
185758384
\end{array}
$$

$$
\begin{array}{r}
185758384 \\
+\ 5 \\
\hline
185758389
\end{array}
$$

$$185758389$$
$$\times 50$$
$$\overline{9287919450}$$

$$9287919450$$
$$+ 49$$
$$\overline{9287919499}$$

$$9287919499$$
$$+ 365$$
$$\overline{9287919864}$$

$$9287919864$$
$$- 615$$
$$\overline{92879192/49}$$

4 The last two numbers in the above sequence—49—represent the volunteer's age and the other numbers are his phone number. Of course, if the second last number is 0, the person playing is under 10 years old and only the last number represents that person's age.

5 This trick is very effective if you can remember the sequence of instructions without referring to a book or notes, and don't be persuaded to repeat the joke to the same group—once will leave them wondering.

You're going to have to move close to the screen to see this one. I'll turn this little FLEA into a DUST MITE!

Did you know?

After television was invented, people began to stay home more. Magicians wanting to perform successfully on this new medium had to create smaller, cleverer tricks.

Trick 67

Spots before your eyes

★ **You need:** a set of dominoes, a piece of paper, a pen, a table

Sleight of hand and good patter will help you perform this trick!

1 Tip out a box of dominoes on the table, but keep one back in your hand. Glance at its spots and write the corresponding numbers on a piece of paper. Hide that domino.

2 Ask a volunteer to lay out all the dominoes, as if you were playing a game.

3 Once this is finished, the numbers at the end of each row will be the same as the numbers you wrote on the piece of paper. Bring the paper out with a flourish.

4 You can do this trick more than once with an audience because you will take a different domino each time, so the answer will always be different. You have to practise keeping a domino hidden of course!

CHAPTER 5

Trick 68
Dinky dice

★ **You need:** three dice, a pen, a piece of paper, a table

When performing this great trick, a smart magician must remember that the opposite sides of a dice always add up to seven.

1 Use a lot of theatrics when performing this trick, because the trick really does itself. Show the audience the three dice, the pen and the paper and ask for a volunteer to help you.

2 While you stand at the back of the stage with your back to the audience, ask the volunteer to roll the three dice, pick them up in any order and stack them one on top of the other.

3 Continue keeping your back to the audience and ask the volunteer to carefully add up the numbers of the five hidden faces of the dice (see illustration). The volunteer now writes down this number and silently shows it to the audience.

4 Once the audience has seen the paper with the number on it, the volunteer should tear it up. Now you should turn around and face the audience. Move to the table and stare at the stacked dice.

5 Bring your hands to your head—pretend that you are concentrating—and announce the correct answer to wild applause!

6 The secret to this trick is that the opposite sides of a dice always add up to seven. You have three dice, so 7 multiplied by 3 equals 21. When you turn and step forward, you look at the number on the top dice, let's say it is 5. Take 5 away from 21 and you get 16. Tell your audience that 16 is the number on the piece of paper—and you'll be absolutely correct.

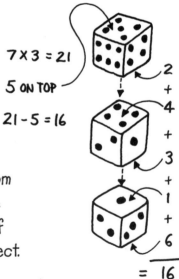

$7 \times 3 = 21$

5 ON TOP

$21 - 5 = 16$

$$\begin{aligned} &2 \\ &+ \\ &4 \\ &+ \\ &3 \\ &+ \\ &1 \\ &+ \\ &6 \\ \hline &= 16 \end{aligned}$$

7 Standing with your back to the audience, having the volunteer tear up the paper and acting as if you were struggling with the answer are all showmanship—the answer is always right in front of you!

Trick 69
Magic dates

★ **You need:** a pen, a piece of paper, an envelope,
a calculator (optional)

This simple but intriguing trick only requires the magician to know what year it is!

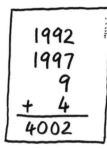

```
1992
1997
   9
+  4
4002
```

1 First things first. Write a figure on the paper and place it in the envelope. Seal it and ask for a volunteer to help with the trick.

2 When the volunteer comes forward, give him the sealed envelope and ask him to keep it in his pocket until you ask for it.

3 Give the volunteer the paper and pen and ask him to write down, then add up, the following four figures:

- ◉ the year he was born
- ◉ the year he began school
- ◉ the age he'll be at the end of this year
- ◉ the number of years since he started school

4 For example, the numbers might look like this:

$$
\begin{array}{r}
1992 \\
1997 \\
9 \\
+\ 4 \\
\hline
4002
\end{array}
$$

5 When the volunteer has finished the addition, ask him to open the envelope. He will be astonished to find that you have already written the same answer and sealed it in the envelope!

6 The secret is that whatever questions you ask your volunteer, you only need to remember the current year! So, as it is 2001, you double that and you will always be right!

7 If you want to ask an adult volunteer some questions, replace 'the year he or she began school' and 'the number of years since he or she started school' with either 'the year he or she began working' and 'the number of years since he or she began working' or 'the year he or she got married' and 'the number of years since he or she got married'. The answer will always be the same—double that of the current year.

Trick 70
Old timers' card trick

★ **You need:** a deck of cards

This is a trick which 'works itself' but you need to keep up the entertaining patter—so practise telling your story before unleashing this on your audience.

 Take any three cards from a full pack of cards, so you now have 49 cards in your hand.

 Ask a member of the audience to come forward and select any card from the pack, memorise it, put it back in the pack

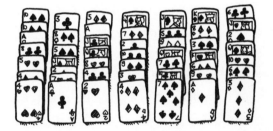

and then shuffle the pack thoroughly. Now, holding the cards face-down, ask your volunteer to deal the cards into seven face-up piles, dealing across the rows each time.

3 Stand well away as the volunteer does this, then ask the volunteer to search each pile until she finds the card she memorised. Numbering the piles from the left to the right, ask her to tell you the number of the pile the card was found in. Once you have this information, ask her to put the piles on top of each other. She should put the second pile on top of the first, the third on top of both, the fourth on top again, and so on.

4 When all the piles are once again assembled into a deck of cards, ask your volunteer to deal out the face-down cards into seven piles of face-up cards in the same way as before. Now request the number of the pile containing the selected card. Mention that you have seen magicians who ask their volunteers to repeat this part of the trick over and over, but you can see that your volunteer is tiring, so twice will be enough.

5 Ask the volunteer to now pile up the cards as before (second pile upon first, and third upon second, and so on) and then ask her to start dealing them out one last time, one by one. After a while, stop her and say the next card will be the one originally chosen. And it will be!

6 How is this so? Well, the secret is simple mathematics— there is a formula in which you can 'predict' the correct card every time! You subtract 1 from the second reported pile number, and multiply this number by 7. Add on the first reported pile number, and the total gives the position of the card in the deck when it is next dealt.

7 So, if the card was in pile five the second time and pile one the first time, the formula would be: $1 - 1 = 0$; $0 \times 7 = 0$; $0 + 5 = 5$, so the fifth card dealt out in the third round will be the chosen card. Often it will be a card in the 20s or 30s which will be the one you are waiting for, so it might be a good idea to practise looking impatient!

Trick 71

Book test

★ **You need:** a paperback book about 180-200 pages long, a playing card or a business card

---

This trick relies on *you* making it look as if you are doing one thing when you are actually doing another!

1 Either hand your own book to an audience member, or ask for a paperback book to be lent to you for the trick—a borrowed book will make your magical skills seem even greater!

2 Ask the audience member to flick through the pages to check each page is different and that the book is genuine and has not been tampered with in any way.

3 Give him the playing card or business card and ask him to turn to any page in the book. Now ask him to look at the page number and the last word on that page and to concentrate hard on them. You should watch and see if he is looking at a right-hand or left-hand page. Now ask your volunteer to insert the playing card or business card into the book and hand it back to you.

4 Now this is the part where you must be seen to be doing one thing, while actually doing another. What you are going to do is chat to the audience about what has happened so far, and while you do this you flick through each

141

and every page of the book, talking about how many thousands of words it must contain. You mention how you need your volunteer to continue to think of the last word on the page he selected, otherwise you'll have little hope of choosing the right word despite your great mental skills.

5 Of course, what you are really doing as you flick through the pages is using the inserted card to your advantage. As you flick your thumb will briefly stop at the page where the card is inserted. Your thumb will jump to the opposite page and in that brief moment you glance down, noting the page number and the last word on either

the right- or left-hand page (depending on which one your volunteer was looking at). You must then continue to flick through the pages, talking all the time about your mental skills and your ability to divine other people's thoughts.

6 Once you know the page number and the last word you should ask your volunteer to try harder to 'send' the correct word to you telepathically. After a suitable length of time, you correctly tell the audience the page number and the last word.

7 This trick really relies on your patter and your ability to keep your audience believing you aren't looking through the book! Make sure you practise this one—it seems easy and it is, but the skill is in making it look very natural.

Trick 72
Linking minds

★ **You need:** a deck of cards (without the jokers), a table

Your audience will believe you really do have magical powers when you perform this trick.

1 All you need to do to prepare for this trick is memorise the top card in the deck.

2 Once your audience arrives, spread the deck out face-down on the table. You must keep track of the top card at all times.

3 Explain that you are going to link minds with a volunteer from the audience. Ask for a volunteer to come up and stand before the table. You will call out the name of a card and she must try and choose the card without looking at the card faces. You need to encourage her by suggesting she take her time and wait until it feels absolutely right.

4 The first card you call out is the card you memorised. Watch to see if your volunteer selects that card. The chances are very good she won't. But whatever card she selects, ask her to hand it to you without looking at it. You

143

now look at it, and say something like, "Not bad," and put it to one side, face-down, so no-one can see it. The next card you call out is the card you have just seen.

5 The volunteer selects another card and hands it to you, after which you assure her she is doing well, and place it face-down on the table with the first card. Call out the name of the just-selected card and the volunteer looks again at the cards, selects one and hands it to you. You again reassure her she is doing well, and say you'll try this time.

6 You name the last card you just looked at and say you'll concentrate on that one. You now reach over and pick up the card you memorised—which was also the first one you named. Put it with the rest and scoop up all the cards chosen.

7 Turn them over one by one for maximum effect to see how you and your volunteer both did. Of course every card is correct.

8 A couple of points. If at any time your volunteer selects the card you initially memorised, end the trick there and turn over all the cards to show they are correct—don't select one yourself. Another good thing is to have another member of the audience write down the cards you call out so you can check them later to prove they are all correct.

★ **You need:** a set of dominoes, a calculator

This trick will show *you* why mathematics is a magician's best friend! Remember it's best not to have to refer to a formula while performing, so memorise the sequence before you begin this trick.

 Spread out the set of dominoes on the table and ask a volunteer to choose one. They should not let you see which one they choose.

 Now give them the calculator and ask them to do the following:

enter one of the domino's numbers	e.g. 4
multiply that number by 5	= 20
add 7 to the total	= 27
double the new total	= 54
add the domino's other number to the result	= 56

 Finally, ask your volunteer to hand the calculator to you with their answer still showing and say you are adding a bit of hocus pocus to find out which domino they chose.

4 As you slowly say the magic words "Ho-cus po-cus", push in "– 14 =" on the calculator, which in the example above would give you an answer of 42—and of course 4 and 2 are the numbers on the chosen domino!

5 If the volunteer had begun their calculation by reversing the numbers (if he began the equation with 2 and added 4 later), the number on the calculator would be 24, as in 2 and 4.

Riveting Rope and Ring Tricks

These tricks are good for young people to perform and for their friends to watch. Ropes and rings are easily obtainable in all lengths and colors, and speciality magic shops sell linking rings and every type of magic rope possible, so clever magicians can vary their tricks.

Trick 74
The absconding ring

★ **You need:** a rope, a ring, a handkerchief

This is a beaut, simple trick to begin a routine. It looks like magic, so it must be magic!

1 First, slip the rope through the ring, just as we've shown in the illustration. Make sure the ends of the rope are knotted together so the ring is trapped.

2 Involve your audience by asking a volunteer to hold the knotted ends while you hold the ring. Use the handkerchief to keep the ring out of sight of the audience.

3 Now tell your audience you will need all your magical powers to free the ring, without untying the rope! Tell the volunteer not to let go of the rope at any cost.

CHAPTER 6

4 Deliver your patter, while you keep your hands out of sight behind the handkerchief. What you are doing with your hands is freeing the knot and pushing the rope downwards over the ring.

SLIDE RING OFF ROPE

5 Utter magical words (whichever ones work best for you) as you free the ring with a flourish, ensuring the rope is still knotted and held by your volunteer—wait for wild applause!

A TRUE MAGICIAN!!

Trick 75
How long?

★ **You need:** a short piece of rope, a longer piece of rope–both the same color and texture

This is another easy to learn and execute rope trick–great to do at the start of a show.

1 You need to prepare your ropes before the audience arrives. Your aim here is for the audience to think you have two ropes of equal length knotted together. That's why the ropes must be the same color and thickness.

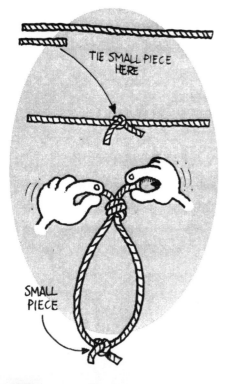

TIE SMALL PIECE HERE

SMALL PIECE

2 First, tie the short piece of rope around the centre of the long piece. Don't tie it too tightly. Tie the two ends of the long piece together as well. Does it look like you now have two pieces of rope of equal length tied together? If not, redo the knots, because that's the most important part of the trick.

3 Now for your performance. Show the ropes to the audience, holding them carefully in both hands. Tell them you are able, because of your exceptional powers, to make these two short pieces of rope into one long piece.

4 Untie the real knotted ends and examine the rope carefully, making sure to mention the knot in the middle of the rope. Now say you're sure you'll be able to get rid of that pesky knot by using a few magic words. In fact, it's a great idea to ask the people in the audience for their favourite magic words and use one or more of them.

THE PESKY KNOT
(The SHORT ROPE)

5 While they are shouting out their magic words, wind the rope around your left hand. Don't stop when you come to the false knot, but actually hide it as you slide it along the longer rope into your right hand.

SLIDE KNOT
ALONG THE
LONG ROPE

SIM SALA BIM!

6 Now is the best time to mutter more magic words and unwind the now completely unknotted rope from your left hand—it's now one piece!

Trick 76

Knots away!

★ **You need:** a length of rope

This is a great close-up trick—and the opposite of the previous trick. Now you should tell your audience you want to create knots...

1 First, put the rope across both hands, with your palms up.

2 Now raise the left hand a little, turning it so the palm actually faces you. Do the same with the right hand and a loop forms.

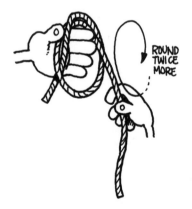

ROUND TWICE MORE

3 Place the loop over your left hand and over the end of the rope which you are holding in your left hand. Allow the rope to pass under your thumb and then return the thumb to its original position.

4 Repeat the looping action twice more and put down the rope (carefully of course!) and build up an air of expectancy with much talk about concentrating otherwise the knots won't appear.

5 Slowly lift the rope and, as you do so, if you have performed the trick correctly, three knots will appear by magic. Remember to speak magic words to make the knots appear faster!

Trick 77
Caught!

★ **You need:** a loop of string, a ring

This is a simple trick, but that doesn't mean it's easy. In this one, you'll catch a ring on a piece of string. You will need to perform a type of throw and flip which needs—yes—practice!

 1 Make sure your audience sits directly in front of you for this trick.

2 Hold the loop of string downward in one hand, stretching it as wide as possible with your fingers spread. Put the ring beneath the loop of string, then bring the ring up, so that the loop of string is inside it. Position the ring about two-thirds of the way up the loop and hold it with your four fingers above it and your thumb below.

3 Now for the tricky bit—the combination throw and flip you have perfected! You need to throw the ring hard down towards the floor, or the bottom of the loop of string, and, at the same time, you need to flip the ring so it turns and catches in a knot at the bottom of the loop.

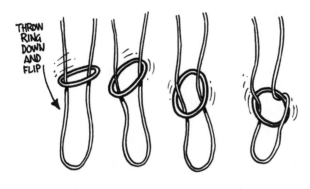

THROW RING DOWN AND FLIP!

4 Once the ring is secured in the knot hold it up to wild applause from your audience.

5 By the way, be prepared to have the ring fall to the floor hundreds of times before you have perfected this trick! Don't give up—it looks wonderful in performance and your friends will love it!

Look old chap... I can make BIG BEN disappear!

I made the STATUE OF LIBERTY vanish for a full 5 minutes!

When did you see Mt FUJI last?

Did you know?

America, Germany, Japan and England have produced world famous magicians. Today, David Copperfield is the magician most people around the world have heard of. He has made a Lear jet disappear! His magic continues to astound.

Trick 78
The disappearing knot

★ **You need:** a piece of thick string (or cord) about 30 cm (12 in.) long, a matchbox cover

This is a terrific trick—your volunteer will believe you can remove a knot from a piece of string and so will the rest of the audience!

1 Using the illustration as a guide, take the string and use it to tie a single knot around the matchbox cover, making sure one end leads off to the right.

2 Hold the matchbox cover upright and poke one loose string end into the centre of the box. Ask a volunteer from your audience to hold the end when it falls through the box.

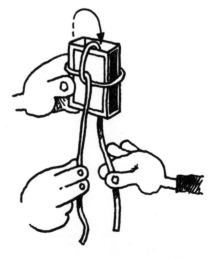

6
CHAPTER

3 Gently—very gently—slide the whole knot off the cover and into the box. Make sure your volunteer is now holding both ends of the string.

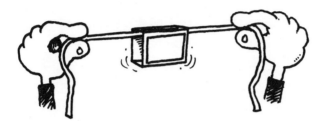

4 Here's where the magic comes in. Grasp the matchbox cover with your left hand, wave your other hand over the top of it, and say several really great magic words, such as "Alikazam!"

5 With you still holding the matchbox cover, ask the volunteer to gently pull apart the ends of the string (which he is still holding of course). You can now slide the matchbox cover up and down the string showing the audience and your volunteer the knot has completely gone!

6 Go so far as to hand the matchbox cover and the string to any audience member who wishes to check your props are genuine!

Trick 79

Rope handcuffs

★ **You need:** two 60 cm (24 in.) lengths of cotton rope

You'll tie your audience up in knots with this trick! (Then you'll free them, of course!)

1 Ask for two brave volunteers. Tie their wrists together with the ropes as shown in the illustration.

2 Now ask them to try really hard to release themselves from their predicament without cutting the rope or untying the knots. Of course they won't be able to do so and now you'll have to help them.

3 First, pull the middle of one of the ropes towards the opposite person so you create a loop. Now draw the loop to the wrist of that person and pass the loop through the rope around the wrist and pull it over the entire hand.

PULL LOOP THROUGH HERE

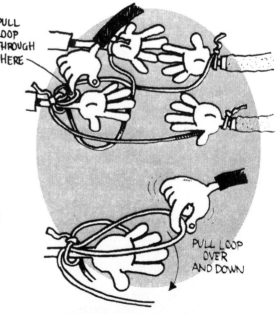

PULL LOOP OVER AND DOWN

4 Once this has occurred you have actually freed your volunteers from their rope handcuffs—ask them to step back from each other and take the wild applause gracefully!

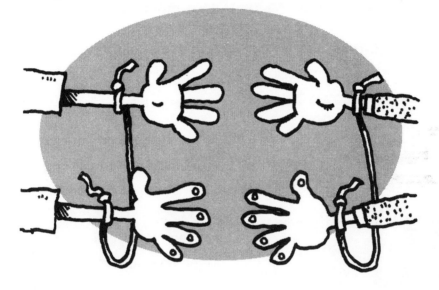

Trick 80
Just one hand

★ **You need:** one length of rope measuring 90 cm (35 in.)

This is another simple trick which audiences love to watch—you'll tie a knot in a rope using just one hand—and they won't know how *you* did it!

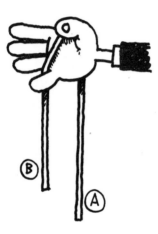

1 Make sure your audience sits directly in front of you. Now drape the rope across your right hand, between the thumb and index finger and behind the little finger. One end needs to be a little longer than the other (see illustration depicting A and B).

2 Give the rope an upward flick and drop your hand down at the same time. You should catch the longer end of the rope (A) between your index and middle fingers.

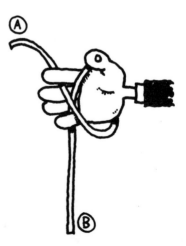

3 Now hold onto the A end of the rope and turn your hand so your fingers are facing the floor. The rest of the rope will slip off your hand, forming a one-handed knot!

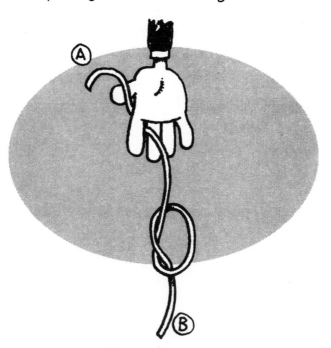

4 You will have to practise that upward flick—but it's worth it, as it's a classy trick when done correctly!

Oooh... Aye ABRACADABRA! I think we might try a wee rabbit here. This haggis is not really doin' the trick!

Did you know?

Pulling a rabbit out of a hat is supposed to be a classic trick. However, it's a trick that is rarely performed. It was probably devised by Scottish magician John Henry Anderson in the 1830s.

Trick 81
Ring release

★ **You need:** a piece of string 45 cm (18 in.) long, a large ring

In this trick, you'll do the seemingly impossible and remove a large ring that's hanging from a piece of string. Think it sounds simple? Not if you can't slip the ring off either end of the string.

1 Once again, your audience needs to be seated directly in front of you for this trick.

2 Slip the large ring on to the string and ask a volunteer to hold one end of the string while you hold the other end. Make sure the string is taut and the ring is in the centre of the string.

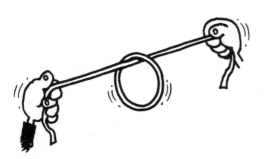

3 Hold the ring at the bottom and turn it once towards you. Explain you are doing this to lock the ring on the string.

6
CHAPTER

4 Now grasp the string where it joins the ring and drop your end of the string. Put this end of the string through the ring.

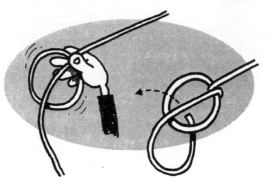

SPIN

5 Again pull the string taut and tell your audience the ring is now 'double locked' on to the string.

6 Grasp the ring and give it a spin. As it stops make sure the string in the centre of the ring is on the bottom. If it isn't, simply turn it until it is.

7 Finally, grasp the ring and move it quickly back and forward on the string as you pull it towards you. The 'locked' ring will come straight off!

163

Trick 82

The prediction pendulum coin

★ **You need:** a piece of string, a coin with a hole,
a large sheet of paper, pencils, a table

You'll know, with the help of your trusty pendulum coin, what
your friends have written!

1 Before your show begins, thread the coin on to
the string.

2 Now for the show—hope
you have a large audience!
Tear the sheet of paper into
eight equally sized pieces and
give the pieces to eight people
in your audience. Ask four people
to write down the name of an
animal and four people to write
down the name of a bird.

RRRIP!

3 One of the volunteers can then spread the pieces
of paper face-down on the table.

4 Hold the string with the coin above the pieces of
paper. Explain to your audience the coin will swing to
and fro over the pieces of paper with animals written on
them, but the coin will circle over the pieces of paper
containing bird names.

5 Now make the coin swing or circle over each piece of paper, according to what you 'see' there, and state whether it's an animal or bird. Immediately turn over the piece of paper to show you're right!

6 You have to be observant and remember two rules when doing this magic trick. First, when you tear the paper, don't use scissors! That's why we said tear it up! The four corner pieces of the sheet of paper will have two smooth edges and two roughly torn edges—these go to the people you ask to write down an animal. The four middle pieces of paper will have three rough edges and one smooth—they go to the people writing birds' names. When you do your pendulum predictions, you only have to remember to swing over the paper pieces with two smooth edges, indicating an animal, and circle over the paper pieces with one smooth edge.

Trick 83
The forever rope

★ **You need:** a piece of rope at least 90 cm (35 in.) long, a table, a wand, a jacket with an inside pocket

Your friends won't mind being strung along with this clever rope trick.

1 Show your audience you are holding a short piece of rope. (In fact, you are holding the ends of your long piece of rope, but more on that later.) Explain that your powers can make the rope grow.

2 Tap the back of one hand with your wand and say some terrific magic words and then begin to pull the rope from one end. It will continue to grow and grow and grow.

3 You can continue to pull the rope, or even better, ask an audience member to do so for you. Once it is coiled on the table, take a bow as your audience applauds.

4 How is it done? It's simple really. Fold the rope in half and make sure both ends are held in your hand. Thread the rest of the rope up your jacket sleeve and into the inside pocket.

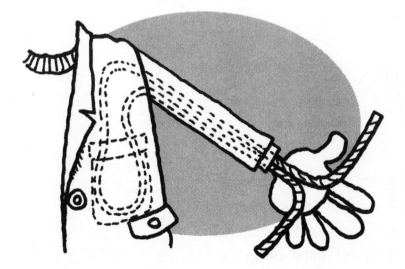

Trick 84
Cut and restored rope

> ★ **You need:** a piece of soft rope about 1.2 m (4 ft) long, scissors

This is a classic trick all magicians need to perfect. You will appear to cut a piece of rope in half, then restore it.

1 Once more, make sure your audience is seated directly in front of you. Drape the centre of the rope over your index finger.

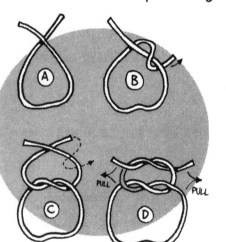

2 Bring one end of the rope up to the middle and tie a square knot.

3 Explain that you have magic scissors, then with a flourish cut the rope. You must cut it in exactly the place shown in the illustration.

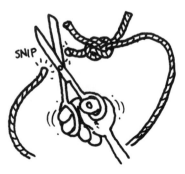

4 Once the cut has been made, casually put the scissors down in a place where the audience cannot see them. Now hold the cotton rope at each end and pull it tightly so everyone can see it's a rope with a knot in the centre.

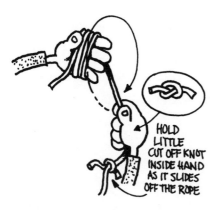

HOLD
LITTLE
CUT OFF KNOT
INSIDE HAND
AS IT SLIDES
OFF THE ROPE

5 Begin to wrap the rope around one of your hands—your left if you are right-handed, your right if you are left-handed. As you wrap the rope, the square knot will slide off the rope and must be concealed in your hand. Reach for your magic scissors, while you quickly drop the piece of rope out of sight.

6 Wave your magic scissors over your wrapped hand and recite your favourite magic words. Put down the scissors—this time in full view of your audience—unwrap the rope and wave it about. The rope is restored!

ABRACADABRA

Trick 85

Two rings and a rope

★ **You need:** two rings, a piece of rope

You cannot get this trick wrong! It's quick and easy to perform and you can dazzle the same audience over and over with your magical skills.

1 First, thread the rope through both rings. Tell the audience there are two ways to take the rings off the rope. One, of course, is to slide the rings to the end of the rope. The other is the magic way! You will show them.

2 Use your left thumb and index finger to hold the rope and one ring really firmly at the point marked A on the illustration. Hold the other ring with your right thumb at point B.

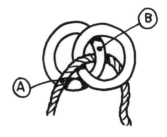

3 Quickly pull your right hand down back towards your body and off the end of the rope. This movement will take the ring which was held in your right hand off the rope. At the same time, you will see the ring held in your left hand miraculously pass through the rope as well!

4 Just await the applause! You can do this trick several times for the same audience—they won't be able to see anything but magic!

Fun with Magic

This is what we hope all your magic tricks
will lead to–lots of fun. There is no real theme
to the following tricks, as there has been with
the ring, rope and coin tricks–in fact, the only
thing they have in common is–yes, you've
guessed it–they're fun!

★ **You need:** ten magazines (or books) with at least 27 pages, a calculator, a table

Yes, you can read minds. You'll prove it with this easy trick.

1 To prepare for this trick, place the magazines in a row on the table and study page 27 in the fourth magazine. Check that page for key words or pictures—anything that is outstanding.

choose
MAGAZINE
Nº 4

2 Give an audience member the calculator and ask her to do the following:

Enter any number between 1 and 100 e.g. 46

Add 28	= 74
Multiply by 6	= 444
Subtract 3	= 441

Divide by 3	= 147
Subtract 3 more than the original number (46 + 3 = 49)	= 98
Add 8	= 106
Subtract 1 less than the original number (46 – 1 = 45)	= 61
Multiply by 7	= 427

The answer will always be 427!

3 Turn your back to your audience and ask your volunteer to look at the first digit of her calculation. She must not tell you what it is, instead she should count out that number of magazines.

My favourite page in the magazine too!

4 Now ask her to look at the final two digits (27) and to turn to that page in the magazine she has chosen. She should hold that page up to show the audience.

5 Ask your volunteer and audience to concentrate on what they can see on the page, so you can read their minds. Of course, you'll have no problems, you have already studied this page! Dazzle your audience by announcing what is on the page!

Trick 87

Faster than a calculator

★ **You need:** a pen or pencil, a piece of paper, a calculator

---

Amaze your friends (and your parents!) by adding up five three-digit numbers in a few seconds, without using a calculator!

1 There is no need to prepare anything for this—you'll use your mental arithmetic skills!

2 Ask a volunteer to write down a three-digit number on the piece of paper. The digits must be different and cannot form a pattern, such as 1, 2, 3.

3 Ask your volunteer to repeat step 2. The three-digit numbers must be different.

4 Ask for one more three-digit number to be written down underneath the first two. This number is the one you are really concerned with—it is the key number.

CHAPTER 7

5 Now you take the pen and paper and write a fourth number. Make sure the sum of the first and fourth numbers equals 999.

6 Write another number, making sure the sum of the second and fifth numbers equals 999.

7 Give the paper back to your volunteer and ask him to use the calculator to add the five numbers—you are not to see the total.

8 Now, when he returns the paper to you (the total is not written on it), pretend to add up the five numbers in your head within seconds. Write down the total. It will match what he has on the calculator.

9 How? Well, remember we said the third number is the key number? It's part of a simple formula, which is:

$$\frac{2000 + (\text{key number} - 2)}{= \text{the answer}}$$

An example:

Volunteer's first number	613
Volunteer's second number	184
Volunteer's third and key number	005
Your number to make 999	086
Your number to make 999	+ 815
	= 2203

$$\frac{2000 + (205 - 2)}{= 2203}$$

10 If your volunteer writes a 9 for the first digit anywhere, add it up to 999, but write down a two-digit number, don't bother with the 0 in front.

2203

Trick 88

In a tearing hurry

★ **You need:** two pieces of paper

This is a quick trick you can only do once for an audience—it's a great show-opener or can be a bit of light relief after a long trick.

1 Before your audience arrives, make two tears in each of the two pieces of paper, creating three equal strips on each sheet. Do not tear through the sheets completely.

2 Once your audience is seated, ask for a volunteer. Hand your volunteer one of the pieces of paper. Ask her to tear away the two end pieces from the middle piece in just one tear. She won't be able to do it, but you can!

3 Pick up the other piece of paper and show her how it's done. Hold one end piece in each hand. Bend over and hold the middle piece with your lips. Now pull the outside pieces, and you will be left with three separate pieces of paper!

Trick 89

The amazing jumping rubber band

★ **You need:** several colored rubber bands

You only have to learn one secret move in order to perform this simple sleight of hand trick, but your audience will think you're an amazing magician!

1 Let the audience see you put a rubber band around two fingers, then you should close your hand.

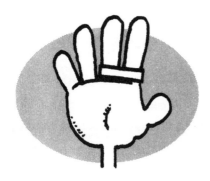

2 As you close your hand, secretly stretch the rubber band and slip all four fingertips inside it. You must do this quickly and secretly. You will need to practise getting all four fingertips into the rubber band with a minimum of movement. Just make it look as if you are making sure your fingers are comfortable. When you look at your hand, you can see the rubber band stretched over the four fingers, but the audience cannot.

3 Open and close your hand. The band automatically (and magically!) jumps to the other two fingers.

4 Of course, now you want to make it jump back again. Put all four fingers into the band as you close your hand; then open and close your hand. See! The band jumps again. It works every time, once you get the hang of it!

5 If you audience is sitting or standing close to you and you want to vary the trick, use two different colored rubber bands and put all four fingertips into both. When you open and close your hand, the bands will magically swap places.

Trick 90

The messy trick

★ **You need: three eggs, three cardboard toilet rolls, one broom, a pie plate, three glasses half-full of water**

In this trick, you're going to make three eggs drop into glasses of water! You'll probably make a mess while you are learning this one—so don't forget to clean up the kitchen when you've finished practising!

 Choose your location—an outside picnic table is a good place to do this trick.

 Allow your audience to stand around, but not too near, the table.

 Set up the trick on the edge of the table. The eggs should sit on top of the cardboard rolls (make sure the eggs are the right size, if they are too small or too large to sit properly on the rolls, the trick won't work), the cardboard rolls should sit on the pie plate, and the pie plate should sit on top of the glasses (see illustration). Check that the pie plate is hanging over the edge of the table.

4 Face the table and place the broom in front of you. The bristles of the broom must be directly below the pie plate. You now step on the bristles while pulling the handle of the broom back towards you.

5 As you let go, the handle of the broom will hit the pie plate straight on and things will fly!

6 The three eggs will fall into the half-full glasses of water! Clever magician!

Trick 91
Stay awake!

★ **You need:** three or four dark-colored balloons, an equal number of light-colored balloons, string, a pin, a wand

You'll keep audiences awake, when you show them how you change the color of a balloon!

1 This trick requires preparation. First, insert your light-colored balloons inside the darker ones. Now inflate each inner (light) balloon, then tie its neck with some string. Secure the same piece of string to the neck of the outer balloon.

2 Now inflate each outer balloon to create an air space between each balloon. Tie the necks of the outer balloons.

3 Attach a pin to the end of your wand—you want to make a bang! Prick one of the outer balloons and your audience will be amazed to see, and hear, it change color.

(If you burst both balloons at once, just tell the members of your audience you thought they looked sleepy and they'll miss the next wonderful trick if they doze off!)

4 Hang the balloons around the stage area so you can easily reach them during a performance. Ensure your audience notices the balloons by referring to them: "I'm surrounded by some fabulous purple balloons, but I do prefer yellow."

5 If you feel the audience is not appreciative enough during any part of your show—touch one of the (outer) balloons with your wand and bang! Not only do people wake up, they realise you've changed the color of the balloon! Burst the balloons throughout your act, ensuring no-one sleeps!

Trick 92
Fruit or vegetable?

★ **You need:** a sheet of paper, three pencils, a hat

Sometimes the simplest tricks are the best. Well, this is one of the best!

1 Prepare for the trick before your audience arrives by tearing a sheet of paper into three equal portions. The trick here is in the tearing—you need to be able to feel the uneven edges of the pieces of paper to enable you to complete the trick. So don't use scissors!

2 Once the audience arrives, ask for three volunteers to come forward to help you with the trick. Hand two volunteers pieces of paper with only one torn edge, that is a piece taken from the end of the original sheet, and ask them to write the name of any fruit on the paper. They are not to show you.

3 At the same time, hand one volunteer the other piece of paper which has two torn sides and ask him to write down the name of a vegetable.

HMMM.... A VEGETABLE

2 TORN SIDES

Try to be casual about which piece of paper you give to each volunteer, but ensure they get the 'right' ones!

4 If you have enough members in the audience, ask a fourth volunteer to come forward and place the three pieces of paper into the hat and mix them up.

5 Tell the audience you are able to pull out only the paper with the vegetable named on it. Now reach into the hat, making a big deal out of the fact you can't see the pieces of paper. Feel quickly for the piece of paper with two torn sides, and voilá! there is your vegetable!

Trick 93
Free-standing pencil

★ **You need:** a pencil with an eraser end, a display pin

Everything you touch is affected by your magic—you'll prove it by making a pencil stand on its own. Or at least that's what your audience will see, as long as you hide the pin at the end of the trick and don't let audience members get too close!

1 Before the show begins, push the pin into the eraser.

2 Stand in front of your audience and hold up the pencil by the eraser. Hide the pin with your fingers. Say something like: "See, it's just an ordinary pencil, but in *my* hands it's a magical thing."

3 Bring up your other hand with its palm facing up and, at the same time, turn your body so the side with the hand holding the pencil is facing the audience.

While you are turning and your fingers are still hiding the pin from view, place the eraser end of the pencil at the base of the middle and ring fingers of your other hand. The pin slides between these fingers and is held in place by your fingers.

 Now here comes the magic! Slowly remove the hand that was originally holding the pencil, preferably while uttering some magic chant, and keep your other hand completely still. It will look as if the pencil is magically standing upright on the palm of your hand.

HOCUS POCUS! SIM SALA BIM!

 After everyone has had their fill of watching the pencil stand for a few moments, remove it (with a flourish and a bow!) and take the pin out with the other hand. Keep the pin hidden in your fingers.

Offer people in the audience a look at the pencil to assure themselves it is just an ordinary pencil.

Trick 94
Soft penetrates hard

★ **You need:** a raw potato with its skin on,
some drinking straws

Most people wouldn't believe a flimsy drinking straw could
pierce a hard, raw potato, but you know better, right?

1 Get straight into this trick by
giving an audience volunteer
the potato and a straw. Challenge her
to push the straw into the potato. She
will fail, so provide her with some
more straws—they'll just
crumple and the potato will
remain unscathed.

2 However, you know how to do this. Take back the
potato and say because you have magical powers,
your drinking straw is stronger than Kryptonite and can
pierce the potato.

3 Fold over the top of
the straw and grip it
tightly in your fist (see
illustration), with the rest of
the straw sticking out.

4 Grip the potato in the palm of your other hand.

5 Chant magical words and 'embrace' your magical powers, then bring down the straw very quickly, powerfully stabbing the potato. Because of the closed top of the straw, the air within is compressed and this makes the straw rigid. Practise until the straw goes through the peel and into the potato.

Trick 95
What a corker!

★ **You need:** two equally sized corks

You'll become a master illusionist with this trick, but be prepared to do many hours of practice! You need to perfect the movements that will convince the audience they are seeing two corks pass through each other!

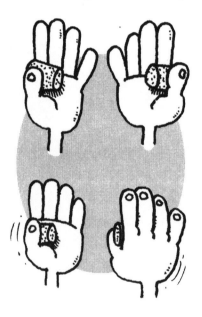

1 Hold one cork in each hand in the crooks between your thumbs and index fingers. Have both palms vertical, so they are facing you.

2 Keep the corks in place but rotate your dominant hand so it is palm down. (If you are right-handed, this will be your right hand, if you are left-handed, it will be your left hand.) Lower the other hand, so it is palm up.

3 The index finger and thumb of your dominant hand (palm down) should now grip the other hand's cork by placing the index finger on the top of the cork and the thumb on the bottom.

4 At the same time, the index finger and the thumb of the other hand (palm up) is gripping the cork of the dominant hand. To do this, the thumb reaches under the fingers of the dominant hand to grip the bottom of the cork, while the index finger reaches under the thumb of the dominant hand to grip the top of the cork. It sounds a lot more complicated than it actually is!

5 Now separate your hands, taking away the opposite corks. As your hands move apart, rotate them again—the hand which was palm down before is now palm up and the hand which was palm up is now palm down.

6 The secret is in practising this moving and rotating. When it's done smoothly, it creates the illusion of the two corks passing through each other—watch it in a mirror while you practise—you'll know when you're ready for an audience.

Trick 96
Coin of illusion

★ **You need:** a pocketful of change

Although you need many coins for this trick—you use none!
Your audience will think you are throwing a coin from hand
to hand, but it's all an illusion!

1 Make a show of taking a handful of coins from your
pocket—let the audience see the coins are real.
Choose one coin and pretend to pick it up—you'll need to
practise this! Return the coins to your pocket.

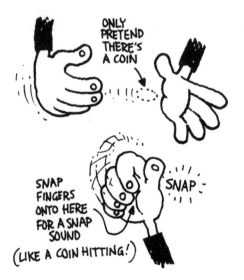

ONLY PRETEND THERE'S A COIN

SNAP FINGERS ONTO HERE FOR A SNAP SOUND
(LIKE A COIN HITTING!)

SNAP

2 Throw the imaginary
coin back and forth
from one hand to the other,
making a small slapping sound
as you pretend to catch the
coin each time. Practise with
a real coin so you can get the
sound right, but if you loosen
your fingers and slap the heel
of your palm as you 'catch'
your coin it should sound OK.

3 Do this several times, then stop and pretend to hold the imaginary coin in one hand. Ask you audience to guess how it landed–"Heads or tails?" Of course, upon opening your hand there is no coin. That's OK because the audience assumes it's now in your other hand.

4 Slowly open your other hand to reveal no coin there either– and bow while your audience applauds!

You should know enough about MAGIC now to know just how I do this trick...!
1 ... 2 .... 3 ...

BANG

Trick 97

How many pieces?

★ **You need:** two strips of paper about 50 cm (20 in.) by 10 cm (4 in.), a black marker pen, glue

---

This is a classic destroy and restore trick!

1 Before your audience arrives, write the words ONE PIECE on each of the two strips of paper. Make the letters look exactly the same on both strips.

2 Fold one strip in half, then in half again, and again, until the paper only measures around 5 cm (2 in.) long and 7.5 cm (3 in.) wide.

3 Glue this tightly folded square to the back of the other strip of paper. Glue it near the end of the strip behind the word ONE.

4 Now, you are ready for an audience. Hold your strip of paper by the ends so the audience sees the words ONE PIECE. Tell your audience you have just the one piece of paper.

194

5 Now tear the strip of paper in half. You must be careful not to expose the paper glued on the back. Place the torn off strip in front of the piece with ONE on it and hold them at the ends.

OR PIECE

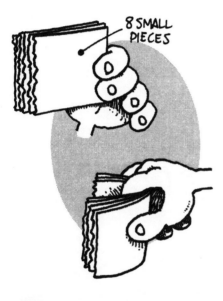

8 SMALL PIECES

6 Say you'd like it smaller, so tear both pieces of paper in half again, putting the pieces on your left side in front of the others again. Tear them one last time—by now making lots of fun of the words ONE PIECE which were written there. You should now have eight pieces.

7 Fold the pieces, keeping the edges away from you and even with the secret folded piece of paper. Are you holding a packet of folded paper between your fingers and thumb of your right hand? You should be. The audience only sees torn pieces of paper but you can see one whole strip.

8 Look confused, and say something like: "But now I've done this, I really think I prefer it as one piece." As you say this, pass the folded packet over to your left hand and turn it around. The strip which is still in one piece should now be facing the audience.

9 Once your fingers and thumb have secured the packet, wave your hand over it and chant a few magic words. Now, dramatically open the strip so the audience can see the words ONE PIECE, apparently whole again!

HOLD TORN PIECES BEHIND HERE

ONE PIECE

10 The torn pieces are folded together so they shouldn't separate and fall to the floor. If they do, keep practising!

Trick 98
Any color

★ **You need:** three different colored crayons, a table

You can choose the correct colored crayon every time—without looking!

1 Prepare for this trick by marking each of the crayons in a different way. You need to be able to tell which crayon is which by just feeling them. The marks, of course, cannot be obvious to anyone looking at the crayons. So, for instance, you might tear a piece of the paper from one, make a nick in the bottom of another with your fingernail or a pair of scissors, and make a nick in the top of the third one. Only you know which mark matches which color, and, naturally, you must remember this!

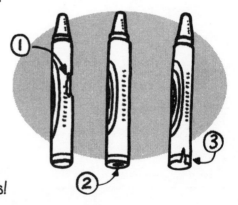

2 With this trick, it's important to be dramatic! You don't want your audience to notice that you are feeling for the mark on a particular crayon, so you need to distract them. Talk to your audience and explain that you're concentrating hard, trying to 'sense' the colors.

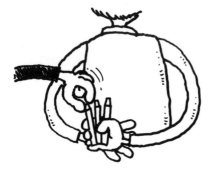

3 To perform the trick, ask a volunteer to randomly place the crayons into your hands, which you are holding behind your back.

4 Now face your audience and ask the volunteer to call out one of the colors. Start acting, while you feel for the mark of the particular color called.

RED

5 When you find the crayon, bring it out with a flourish and wait for the applause. Only do this trick once or twice in a show.

THAT LOOKS LIKE RED TO ME...! DO I HAVE EYES ON THE BACK OF MY HEAD..? YOU ASK.

Trick 99

Hidey ho

★ **You need:** a deck of cards, a large scarf
(or handkerchief)

You're such a good magician that any card you name can penetrate a solid object, such as a scarf!

1 All you have to do beforehand is secretly memorise the top card in the deck and then remember not to shuffle the cards!

MEMORISED CARD NOW ON BOTTOM OF PACK

2 Hold the deck face-up in the palm of your left hand if you're right-handed, or in your right if you are left-handed. The card you have memorised should be sitting on the bottom of the pack in your palm.

3 Show the scarf to the audience—in fact, pass it around so everyone can see it's an ordinary scarf.

4 Once it's returned to you, drape the scarf over the pack of cards so its centre rests on top of the deck.

5 Make sure you draw the audience's attention to the fact you can't see the cards because the scarf is covering the pack. Now, reach under the scarf with your other hand and remove the deck, but leave the memorised card behind in your palm.

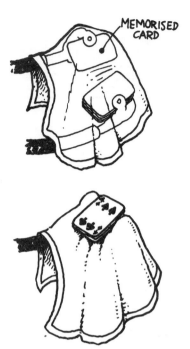

MEMORISED CARD

6 Place the deck of cards on top of the scarf, directly over the card that is hidden under the scarf.

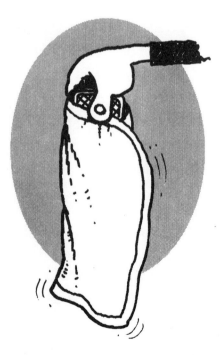

7 Begin to wrap the deck of cards in the scarf. Start by folding the edge nearest you away from you with your free hand. Place the thumb of this hand underneath the card in your opposite palm and the wrapped deck. Place the rest of the fingers of that hand on top to grip the deck, and now revolve it upright so the hidden card faces you. Do this part carefully, because if you allow the hidden card to shift the audience will see it!

8 Now, keeping the hand gripping the package where it is, use your opposite hand to fold the sides of the scarf back towards you, diagonally over the hidden card. The folds need to overlap this card, while your thumb holds everything in place.

9 It's time to dazzle your audience! With the fist of the hand that folded the scarf, grip all of the scarf hanging below and rotate the deck (keeping the hidden card facing you) so it is hanging down. If the folds are tight enough, the hidden card should stay in place when you lift your thumb.

10 Tell your audience that you can magically make any card you call appear through the scarf. Now, of course, you call to the card you have memorised—the hidden card—and then shake the deck, while chanting magic words. The hidden card will magically begin to appear as if it is penetrating the centre of the scarf. When it hits the table, allow the wrapped deck to be examined as you are basking in your audience's admiration!

SHAKE SHAKE

Trick 100
Counting cards

★ **You need:** a deck of cards

This is a simple 'find the card' trick that works on its own, but you can make it yours with some cleverly planned patter.

10 CARDS

1 Count out the top 10 cards from a pack of cards, but don't let your audience guess that you are counting. Use some patter to distract the audience while you set up the trick.

2 When you've counted out 10 cards, sweep them up and return them to the top of the deck, secretly glancing at the bottom card—let's say it's the eight of clubs.

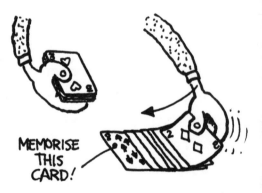

MEMORISE THIS CARD!

3 Ask the audience, or a particular person in the audience, for a number between 10 and 20. (If the number nominated is 20, the trick won't work so you need to stress you need a number between 10 and 20.) If the number you're given is say, 14, you count out 14 cards on to the table.

14 CARDS

4 Put the rest of the pack to one side and add the digits of the chosen number, 1 and 4, together. You get 5.

5 Deal out five cards from the packet and the fifth card will be the eight of clubs!

SMALL PILE

CARD Nº 5 will be 8 of SPADES

Trick 101
A no-card card trick

★ **You need:** a deck of cards, nothing but your mind, and some good patter

Finally, here's a card trick you can perform when you don't have a pack of cards handy.

1 Ask an audience member to name a number between one and ten, then tell him he should change his mind and choose another number! He mustn't tell anyone the second number, but ask him to double it.

2 Now, ask him to add 14 to it; then divide by 2; then subtract the original number. The answer is the value of his imaginary card. He must remember it.

3 For example:

First choice	3
Second number	4
Double it	8
Add 14	22
Divide by 2	11
Subtract original (– 4)	7

4 Now ask him to concentrate on a suit of cards—either hearts, clubs, diamonds or spades. You pretend to concentrate and then blurt out a suit, for instance, "Diamonds."

5 It is unlikely your first guess will be right, so keep guessing until you name the right suit.

6 Of course, the audience now thinks you're having trouble with the trick, as you probably took a few guesses to get the right suit. But, as soon as you guess the suit, you say something like: "Boy, I can't believe you chose the seven of hearts (or whatever)."

7 Pause here, you need your volunteer to realise you have chosen the correct value of the card and for him to tell the audience how clever you are.

8 This is really a simple trick. If you ask your volunteer to add 14, the final number will be 7; if you ask him to add 10, the final number will be 5, and so on. The answer is always going to be half of the number you ask him to add.

You're the greatest magician I know!